FROM THE DEPTHS TO THE HEIGHTS

A Young Person's Journey of Faith

By Rev. Cleon J. Alleyne

First Edition
Published by Depths to Heights

DEDICATION

ACKNOWLEDGMENTS

I am deeply grateful for the many people who have walked alongside me on this incredible journey of faith. This book would not have been possible without your love, support, and encouragement.

First, I thank God for His constant guidance, grace, and love. Every step of this journey has been directed by His hand, and I give Him all the glory for the stories and lessons shared in this book.

To my family, thank you for being my rock and foundation. Your love and prayers have strengthened me through every trial and triumph. I especially want to honor my late mother and brother—your love and faith continue to inspire me every day.

To my foster son, Vilson Havdia, your joy, and heart for God have been a light in my life. Thank you for walking this path of faith with me.

I want to extend my deepest gratitude to my dear friends who have stood by me and believed in this project: Robin Stephen, Aaron Jääskeläinen, Mark Moses, Vesa Holappa, Sherry Simpson, and Beth Prophitt. Your friendship, prayers, and encouragement have carried me through many seasons, and I am so blessed to know you.

Thank you to the countless people I have met on the mission field, Guyana, Albania, Finland, and beyond. Each of you has impacted my life and ministry in ways I cannot fully express. You have shown me what it means to serve God with your whole heart.

Lastly, thank you to the young readers of this book. My prayer is that the stories and lessons shared here inspire you to follow God with all your heart, trusting Him in every step of your journey.

PREFACE

The journey of faith is filled with highs and lows, victories, and challenges, but through it all, one thing remains constant—God's love for us. I authored this book, "From the Depths to the Heights: A Young Person's Journey of Faith," to share the incredible ways that God has worked in my life, from my early days in Guyana to my missionary work in Albania and Finland. Along the way, I have experienced moments of boundless joy, deep sorrow, and everything in between, but each step has drawn me closer to God.

This book is written especially for young people like you, who are just beginning your journey with God. When I was 13 years old, I first heard God's call on my life, and it changed everything. I did not have all the answers, and there were times when I felt afraid, unsure, or even lost. But through it all, God was with me, guiding my steps and showing me His plan for my life. My hope is that by reading these stories and lessons, you will be encouraged to trust God in your own journey—no matter where He is leading you.

You will read about the challenges I faced, the lessons I learned, and the incredible ways God revealed His love and faithfulness to me. I pray that these stories will

inspire you to step out in faith, even when it is hard, and to live for God every day.

Whether you are just beginning to follow Jesus, or you have been walking with Him for a while, I want you to know this: God has an amazing plan for your life. He is calling you to do wonderful things, and when you trust Him, there is no limit to what He can do through you.

As you read this book, may you be reminded that you are never too young to make a difference. God can use you, right where you are, to share His love and to live a life full of purpose and adventure. So, let us begin this journey together—from the depths of life's challenges to the heights of God's calling.

TABLE OF CONTENTS

INTRODUCTION

Welcome! I am so excited that you have picked up this book, because what you are about to read could change your life forever. You may not realize it yet, but God has an incredible plan for you. No matter how young or old you are, He is calling you to follow Him, to trust Him, and to live a life full of purpose, love, and adventure.

I want to share with you some of the lessons I have learned on my own journey with God. I did not always know what He had in store for me, but from an early age, I knew I wanted to follow Him. When I was just 13 years old, living in Guyana, I felt God calling me to give my life to Him. That decision set me on a path I never could have imagined—one that took me to places like Albania and Finland, and allowed me to serve as a missionary, sharing God's love with people all over the world.

But let me be honest with you: it was not always easy. There were times when I felt afraid, times when I did not understand what God was doing, and times when I wanted to give up. But through every challenge, God was with me, guiding me, and giving me the strength to keep going.

In this book, I will share some of those stories—stories of faith, friendship, struggles, forgiveness, and learning to trust God when life does not make sense. These are not just my stories; they are lessons that you can apply to your own life. I believe that the same God who called me when I was young is calling you, too. He has a special plan for your life, and He wants you to be a part of His great mission.

As you read, I hope you will be encouraged to follow Jesus with all your heart, to trust Him when things are tough, and to live boldly for Him every day. You do not have to have all the answers right now. You just need to be willing to take that first step of faith and say, "Here I am, Lord. Send me."

So, let us begin this journey together. I pray that as you read these pages, God will speak to your heart, remind you of His love, and inspire you to live for Him in everything you do. The adventure is just beginning!

Chapter 1

HEARING GOD'S CALL EARLY

The hot, humid air of Guyana wrapped around me as I sat quietly in the back row of the small, bustling church. I was 13 years old, just a boy, but something about that evening felt different. I had been to church so many times before—so many Sundays spent sitting through services with my family—but this night was different. As I listened to the pastor speak, his words did not just float over me like they usually did. Instead, they seemed to sink deep into my heart, each one hitting like an arrow of truth.

He spoke about God's call. He talked about how God was not just looking for the grown-ups in the room, but for the young too—how God could use anyone, no matter their age, if they were willing to follow Him. His words stirred something inside me. I did not know what it was at the time, but it felt like God was calling me—me, a young boy from Guyana with no grand plans for the future.

I thought about it the whole evening. Could God really be calling me? What could He want with someone like me? I was not important or special; I was just a boy. The doubt whispered to me, telling me I was too young, too inexperienced. But the pull in my heart was undeniable.

At the end of the service, the pastor invited anyone who felt that call to come forward and commit their lives to Jesus. My heart pounded in my chest. I felt a rush of nervousness, but I knew I could not stay in my seat. Slowly, I stood up and walked to the front, each step feeling like a leap into the unknown. Kneeling at the altar, I whispered a simple prayer, asking Jesus into my life.

From that night onward, everything changed. Church was not just a routine anymore—it became a place where I could connect with God, where I felt His presence. I still did not have all the answers, but I knew that God had something special for me, even if I could not see the whole picture yet.

Looking back now, I realize that night was the beginning of an incredible journey—one that would take me from the small streets of Guyana to places I could never have imagined. It was proof that God's call can come at any age, and when we say yes to Him, He leads us on an adventure greater than anything we could plan for ourselves.

Reflection Verse

"Before I formed you in the womb, I knew you, before you were born, I set you apart; I appointed you as a prophet to the nations."

*— **Jeremiah 1:5 (NIV)***

Reflection

Have you ever felt that God is calling you to something special? It can be a quiet tug in your heart, like it was for me, or a more obvious moment when you know God is speaking to you. One thing is for sure: it does not matter how young or old you are—God has a plan for your life.

In the Bible, we read about Jeremiah, who was called by God even before he was born. That same God who knew Jeremiah and called him is the same God who knows and calls you. He has a unique purpose for your life, and all you need to do is trust Him and say yes to His call, no matter how unsure you might feel.

Prayer

Dear God,

Thank You for calling me, even when I feel too young or not ready. Help me to hear Your voice and trust in Your plan for my life. I want to follow You and step into the adventure You have prepared for me. Give me courage, Lord, and help me to say yes to You, no matter what.

Amen.

Take sometime this week to think about how God might be calling you. Is there something you feel He is asking you to do? Maybe it's a small step, like praying more or helping someone in need. Or perhaps it's something bigger, like sharing your faith with a friend. Whatever it is, write it down and pray for the courage to say yes, just like I did when I was 13.

*Also, reflect on **Jeremiah 1:5** and think about how God has known you and had a plan for your life, even before you were born. How does that truth make you feel?*

Chapter 2

FAITH OVER FEAR

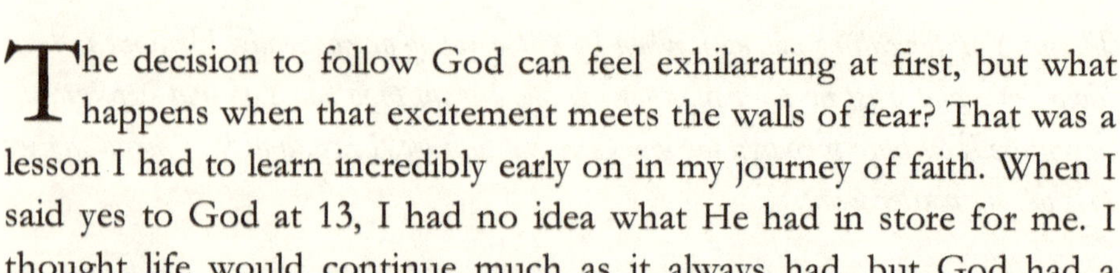

The decision to follow God can feel exhilarating at first, but what happens when that excitement meets the walls of fear? That was a lesson I had to learn incredibly early on in my journey of faith. When I said yes to God at 13, I had no idea what He had in store for me. I thought life would continue much as it always had, but God had a different plan—a plan that required me to step out of my comfort zone and confront fears I did not even know I had.

Not long after I committed my life to Jesus, I began hearing stories about missionaries—people who traveled far from home to share the Gospel with those who had never heard it. The idea both thrilled and terrified me. The thought of going on a mission was exciting, but it also brought fear: the fear of the unknown, the fear of leaving my family, and the fear of not being good enough to do what God might be asking of me.

At first, I dismissed the idea. I was just a teenager. Surely, God was not calling me to leave my home in Guyana and go off to some faraway place to tell others about Jesus. That was for other people, for adults who had it all figured out—not for me. But the more I prayed, the more I felt the nudge of the Holy Spirit urging me to take a step of faith.

That nudge became even stronger when a friend told me about an organization called Youth With A Mission (YWAM). YWAM was known for sending young people on missions to countries all around the world, and my friend suggested I get involved. As soon as She mentioned it, I felt my heart race with both excitement and fear. Could I really do something like that? Could I leave behind everything I knew—my family, my home, the familiar comfort of daily life—to follow God into the unknown?

For weeks, I wrestled with the idea. The fear of failure loomed large in my mind. What if I was not good enough? What if I did not know what to say or do when I got there? What if people did not listen to me? The doubts swirled, threatening to drown out the call I felt deep in my heart.

Then one Sunday, during a church service, the pastor spoke about the story of Peter walking on water. He reminded us how Peter, at the sound of Jesus' voice, stepped out of the boat and into the stormy waters. Peter did not have all the answers; he did not even know if he would sink or swim. But he stepped out in faith, trusting that Jesus would be there to catch him if he fell. And in that moment, I knew what I had to do. Like Peter, I did not have all the answers, but I knew God was calling me to take that first step of faith, even if fear stood in the way.

I went home that day and prayed earnestly, asking God to give me the courage to face my fears. And slowly, peace began to replace the fear. I realized that God was not asking me to be perfect; He was simply asking me to trust Him. So, with trembling hands but a heart full of faith, I signed up to join YWAM.

The first mission trip I went on was to a remote village in Guyana. It was not far from home, but for a young boy who had never done anything like this before, it felt like stepping into a whole new world. As soon as we arrived, I could feel my fears rising to the surface. The village was unfamiliar, the people were strangers, and I felt completely out of my depth. What if I said the wrong thing? What if no one wanted to hear about Jesus?

On the first night, we gathered in the village center, where we were going to share a message of hope with the people. I could feel the weight of the moment pressing down on me as we prepared to speak. My heart pounded in my chest, and my mouth went dry. What if I could not do this?

But then, as I stood there, I remembered Peter stepping out of the boat. I remembered that this was not about me or my abilities. It was about God working through me. I whispered a simple prayer: "Lord, help me to trust You." And in that moment, something incredible happened. As I began to speak, I felt a surge of confidence—not in myself, but in God. The words flowed out of me, and I could feel the presence of the Holy Spirit guiding me.

The people in the village listened, and by the end of the night, several of them came forward to accept Jesus into their lives. I was in awe—not of what I had done, but of what God had done through me, despite my fears.

That mission trip was just the beginning. Over the years, God would continue to call me to step out in faith, even when fear was knocking at the door. Each time I faced that fear, I learned more about trusting God. I learned that fear does not have to stop us; it is just an obstacle that we can overcome with God's help.

Reflection Verse

"So do not fear, for I am with you; do not be dismayed, for I am your God. I will strengthen you and help you; I will uphold you with my righteous right hand."

— Isaiah 41:10 (NIV)

Reflection

Fear is something we all face. Whether it is fear of the unknown, fear of failure, or fear of stepping out of our comfort zone, it can feel overwhelming. But the good news is that God promises to be with us through it all. When we trust Him, we can find the strength to take that first step, just like Peter did when he stepped out of the boat. It is not about having all the answers or being perfect—it is about trusting that God will uphold us with His strength.

What fears are you facing right now? Is there something God is calling you to do that feels scary or uncertain? Remember, you do not have to do it alone. God is with you, and He will give you the strength you need.

Prayer

Dear God,

Thank You for always being with me, even when I am afraid. Help me to trust You more and to take steps of faith, even when fear tries to hold me back. I know that You are bigger than any fear I face, and I believe that You will strengthen me and guide me, just as You have promised. Thank You for Your unfailing love and support.

Amen.

Take a piece of paper and write down one fear that is holding you back from following God's call. It could be a fear of failure, fear of what others might think, or even fear of stepping into the unknown. After you write it down, pray and ask God to help you overcome that fear. Then, tear up the paper as a symbol of letting go of your fear and trusting God's plan for your life.

Also, memorize **Isaiah 41:10** *and remind yourself of this verse whenever fear tries to take hold. Let it be a constant reminder that God is with you, and He will give you the strength you need to step out in faith.*

Chapter 3

SERVING OTHERS WITH LOVE

When I first became a missionary, I had this idea that serving God would mean doing big, dramatic things—preaching to crowds, leading people to Christ in droves, and transforming entire communities. But God had other lessons for me to learn, ones that went far beyond the big moments. One of the most important lessons was about love—the kind of love that is lived out in small, simple acts of service.

My first mission work was not in some far-off country. It was right there in my home of Guyana. I had just joined Youth With A Mission (YWAM), eager to start making a difference for God. I was ready to take on the world, but God's plan was to show me that serving others is not just about doing grandiose things—it is about meeting people where they are and loving them in the small, everyday moments.

One day, we were sent to visit a family that lived in one of the poorest parts of the city. I will never forget the moment we arrived at their home. The house was small and rundown, with barely enough space for the family inside. The children's clothes were worn and dirty, and their eyes reflected the struggles they had faced in life. My heart broke as I looked around at the conditions they were living in.

We sat with the family, talking, and listening to their story. They had faced hardship after hardship, struggling just to make it through each day. I wanted so desperately to do something big, something that would fix everything for them. But I quickly realized that I did not have the resources to change their situation overnight. What could I possibly do for them?

That is when God taught me a powerful lesson. As we sat with the family, we prayed with them. We shared the love of Jesus, not through grand gestures, but through simple kindness—listening, comforting, and offering a glimmer of hope. The family did not need someone to fix all their problems right away. What they needed was love—the love of Christ shown through us, in small ways, with no strings attached.

At first, I wondered if what we were doing was enough. I wanted to do more. But as we prayed with that family, I saw something change. Tears filled their eyes, not because we had solved all their problems, but because they felt seen and loved. They knew that someone cared for them, that God cared for them.

That day, I learned that serving others is not about doing the biggest or flashiest thing. It is about showing love in whatever way you can, even if it is as simple as sitting with someone, listening to their story, and praying with them. Those small acts of kindness can make an enormous difference in someone's life. They can remind people that they are not alone, that God sees them and cares for them.

As my journey continued, God gave me more opportunities to serve in diverse ways. I traveled to Albania and Finland, working with people from all walks of life—children, the elderly, the sick, and the poor. Each time, I was reminded that serving is not about the size of the act, but the heart behind it. Whether we are offering a meal to someone in need, praying for a friend, or simply spending time with someone who feels lonely, we are showing the love of God.

In Albania, I saw this lesson play out in a powerful way. We were working with street children in Tirana, many of whom had been abandoned or neglected. They were homeless, begging for food, and often faced harsh conditions. As a team, we organized activities for them—games, lessons, and meals—but what I realized was that what these children needed most was not just material help. They needed love, someone to care for them and see them as valuable.

One day, we were playing a simple game of soccer with the children. For a moment, I saw the joy in their eyes, the way they laughed and played without a care in the world. It was a small thing—just a game—but it was more than that. It was a chance for these children to feel like they mattered, like someone cared enough to spend time with them. And in that moment, I realized that sometimes the simplest acts of love are the most powerful.

As followers of Jesus, we are called to serve others, not because we must, but because we want to show the love of Christ. Jesus Himself said that He came not to be served, but to serve, and to give His life as a ransom for many. If our Savior, the Son of God, came to serve, then how much more should we be willing to serve others with love and humility?

Every act of service, no matter how small, is an opportunity to show the love of God to the world. It is a chance to be His hands and feet, meeting people where they are and loving them in the way Jesus loves us. And when we do that, we reflect the heart of God in the most beautiful way.

Reflection Verse

"Each of you should use whatever gift you have received to serve others, as faithful stewards of God's grace in its various forms."

— *1 Peter 4:10 (NIV)*

Reflection

Serving others is one of the greatest ways we can show God's love. But serving is not always about doing big, noticeable things. It is about the small, everyday acts of kindness that touch people's hearts and remind them that they are loved by God.

How can you serve others in your life? Maybe it's helping a friend who is having a tough day, offering to pray for someone, or even doing something simple like spending time with someone who feels lonely. When you serve with love, you are being a faithful steward of God's grace.

Prayer

Dear God,

Thank You for teaching me what it means to serve others with love. Help me to use the gifts You have given me to show Your love to the people around me. Whether in big or small ways, I want to be a reflection of Your heart. Teach me to serve with humility, knowing that even the simplest acts of kindness can make a difference. Thank You for the privilege of being part of Your mission to love and care for others.

Amen.

This week, find one way to serve someone in your life. It does not have to be something big—maybe it's helping a friend with a chore, offering to listen to someone who is going through a hard time, or praying for someone in need. After you do it, reflect on how it felt to serve with love. Did you see God working through that act of kindness?

*Also, spend time reflecting on **1 Peter 4:10** and think about the gifts God has given you. How can you use those gifts to serve others? Write down a few ideas and pray for opportunities to put them into action.*

Chapter 4

FACING HARDSHIP AND REJECTION

One of the hardest lessons I had to learn as a young missionary was that following Jesus did not mean everything would go smoothly. In fact, there were times when my faith was tested in ways I never imagined. One of the most difficult trials came in the form of hardship and rejection—not from strangers, but from people I had grown to trust and care about.

After serving in Guyana for several years, God opened the door for me to go to Albania, a country that had only recently emerged from decades of communist rule. Albania's past had left deep scars, and for years, religion had been outlawed, and churches had been forced underground. When I arrived, I was filled with excitement and hope, ready to share the love of Jesus with people who desperately needed to hear it.

But what I did not expect was how difficult that task would be.

At first, things went well. We connected with local churches, organized events for young people, and began to build relationships in the community. But as time went on, I began to notice a resistance, an underlying suspicion toward foreigners, especially missionaries. Many people were wary of us, unsure of our intentions, and some outright rejected the message we brought.

One of the most painful moments came when I met a young man named Arben. He was one of the first people I had befriended in Albania. We spent countless hours talking about life, faith, and everything in between. Arben seemed eager to learn more about Jesus, and I could see that God was stirring something in his heart. I poured my time and energy into mentoring him, hoping that he would soon make a decision to follow Christ.

But just as our friendship was deepening, things took a turn. One day, Arben stopped responding to my calls and messages. He became distant, and I could not understand why. After weeks of silence, I learned the truth—his family, devout in their own cultural beliefs, had pressured him to cut ties with me. They were afraid that his association with a foreign missionary would bring shame or trouble to their household.

I was crushed. It was not just the loss of a friend that hurt—it was the rejection of the very message I had come to share. I questioned myself: Had I done something wrong? Had I pushed too hard? The sting of rejection was real, and for a while, it made me question whether I was even meant to be in Albania.

But God had a lesson for me in that painful experience. As I sat in prayer one evening, pouring out my frustration and heartache to God, He reminded me of something: Jesus Himself faced rejection. He was rejected by His own people; misunderstood by the very ones He came to save. If Jesus, the Son of God, was rejected, then I should not be surprised when I face rejection for sharing His message.

In that moment, I realized that rejection was not a sign that I had failed. It was simply part of the journey. Jesus never promised that following Him would be easy. In fact, He warned His disciples that they would face hardship and persecution because of their faith. But He also promised something greater—that He would be with us through every trial.

I began to see the rejection I faced in a new light. Instead of letting it discourage me, I allowed it to deepen my dependence on God. I prayed more fervently, asking God to soften the hearts of the people I was trying to reach. And over time, I saw God work in ways I never expected.

One day, as I was walking through a village in the hills of Albania, a young boy ran up to me. He had heard me speak at a youth event weeks earlier, and he wanted to know more about Jesus. His curiosity was genuine, and as we talked, I realized that God was still at work, even when I could not see it. The rejection I had faced was not the end of the story—it was just part of the process.

That experience taught me that following Jesus means persevering through hardship and rejection. It means trusting that even when doors close, God is still opening others. And it means knowing that every seed we plant, even if it seems to fall on hard soil, has the potential to grow in ways we may never see.

Reflection Verse

"Blessed are those who are persecuted because of righteousness, for theirs is the kingdom of heaven."

— Matthew 5:10 (NIV)

Reflection

Have you ever experienced rejection for your faith or beliefs? It is never easy to face, especially when it comes from people you care about. But Jesus reminds us that when we face hardship or persecution for His sake, we are blessed. Our reward is not in the approval of others, but in the knowledge that we are walking in God's will.

Rejection does not mean we have failed. Sometimes it is a sign that we are on the right path. God calls us to persevere, even when things are hard, trusting that He is at work behind the scenes. How can you trust God more when you face rejection or hardship in your life?

Prayer

Dear God,

Thank You for reminding me that even when I face rejection, you are still with me. Help me to trust You more and to stand firm in my faith, even when it is hard. Give me the strength to persevere through hardship, knowing that You are at work in ways I cannot always see. I pray that You would soften the hearts of those who have rejected You and that Your love would reach them in ways beyond my understanding. Amen.

Think about a time when you experienced rejection—whether it was because of your faith or something else in your life. How did it make you feel? Take a moment to write about that experience in a journal or talk to someone you trust about it. Then, spend some time in prayer, asking God to give you the strength to keep going, even when you feel discouraged.

Also, memorize **Matthew 5:10** *and remember that God promises to bless those who persevere through persecution and hardship for His sake.*

Chapter 5

THE POWER OF FRIENDSHIP

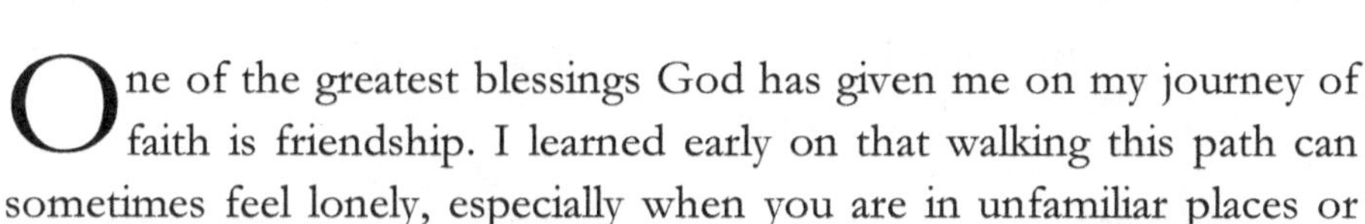

One of the greatest blessings God has given me on my journey of faith is friendship. I learned early on that walking this path can sometimes feel lonely, especially when you are in unfamiliar places or facing challenges. But God never intended for us to walk alone. He designed us to be part of a community, to have friends who encourage us, pray for us, and walk with us through the highs and the lows.

When I first moved to Albania, I did not know anyone. I was excited about the adventure, but as the days went by, I started to feel the weight of being far from home, in a place where I did not speak the language, and where the culture was vastly different from what I was used to. It was in those moments that God brought incredible friends into my life—people who became like family and who helped me grow in ways I could never have imagined.

One of those friends was Sean, a fellow missionary from America. Sean and I met early in my time there, and from the start, we clicked. Despite our different backgrounds, we shared the same heart for God and the same passion for ministry. Sean's joy and love for God were infectious, and his friendship quickly became a lifeline for me. We would often stay up late, talking about our faith, our struggles, and our dreams for the future. In those conversations, I found strength and encouragement to keep going, even when things were tough.

There was one evening in particular that stands out in my mind. I had been struggling with a tricky situation in the ministry, feeling discouraged and unsure of how to move forward. I felt like I was failing, like I was not making the impact I had hoped for. I was on the verge of giving up.

That night, Sean invited me over for dinner. We sat at his small kitchen table, sharing a simple meal, and as we talked, I opened up about what I was going through. Sean listened patiently, nodding as I poured out my heart. Then, with a calm and steady voice, he reminded me of something I had forgotten: "Cleon, it is not about the results we see right now. It is about being faithful to what God has called us to do. We plant the seeds, but it is God who makes them grow."

His words hit me like a bolt of lightning. I had been so focused on what I could see—the challenges, the lack of immediate results—that I had forgotten the bigger picture. Sean's friendship was a gift in that moment, a reminder that I was not alone and that God was still at work, even when I could not see it.

We prayed together that night, asking God for strength and wisdom, and I left his home with a renewed sense of purpose. From that day forward, Sean and I became even closer. We prayed for each other, encouraged each other, and held each other accountable in our faith. His friendship taught me that we all need people in our lives who will point us back to God when we lose our way.

God brought other amazing friends into my life as well, each one playing a unique role in my journey. When I later moved to Finland, I met Aaron, a young man from my church in Oulu. Like Sean, Aaron and I connected quickly, and his friendship became a source of joy and laughter during my time there. Aaron was someone I could count on for honest conversations, and he was not afraid to challenge me when I needed it. But he also knew how to encourage me when I was struggling. We spent hours walking through the Finnish wilderness, talking about life, faith, and everything in between. Aaron had a way of making me see the beauty in the simple moments, reminding me that God's presence is everywhere, even in the quiet places.

Another friend who became a pillar of strength for me in Finland was Vesa. Vesa was one of the first people I met when I arrived in Finland, and from the moment we met, he welcomed me with open arms. Vesa's kindness and generosity were unmatched, and his friendship made the cold Finnish winters a little warmer. We spent countless evenings talking about our shared love for God and our desire to see His kingdom grow. Vesa's friendship was not just about having someone to hang out with—it was about having someone who truly understood the challenges of ministry and who was always there to offer a listening ear and a word of encouragement.

Looking back, I realize that these friendships were more than just a comfort—they were lifelines. They reminded me that no matter how hard the journey became, I was not walking it alone. God had placed these people in my life for a reason, to strengthen me, encourage me, and remind me of His faithfulness.

The power of friendship in the Christian life cannot be overstated. We are meant to bear one another's burdens, to lift each other up when we fall, and to celebrate the victories together. I have learned that God often speaks to us through the friends He brings into our lives, using them to point us back to Him when we lose sight of His promises.

Whether it was Sean in Albania, Aaron and Vesa in Finland, or the countless other friends God has placed in my life, each one has played a crucial role in helping me stay the course. They have been the hands and feet of Jesus to me, and I am forever grateful for the ways they have shaped my journey of faith.

Reflection Verse

"A friend loves at all times, and a brother is born for a time of adversity."

— Proverbs 17:17 (NIV)

Reflection

Friendship is one of the most beautiful gifts God gives us. As Christians, we are called to walk together, supporting one another through the ups and downs of life. We need friends who will remind us of God's faithfulness when we feel discouraged, who will pray with us when we are struggling, and who will celebrate with us in times of joy.

Think about the friends God has placed in your life. Who are the people who have encouraged you, prayed for you, and helped you grow in your faith? Take a moment to thank God for them and ask Him to help you be that kind of friend to others as well.

Prayer

Dear God,

Thank You for the gift of friendship. I am so grateful for the friends You have placed in my life, the ones who have encouraged me, supported me, and reminded me of Your love. Help me to be the kind of friend who points others to You, who listens, prays, and loves with the heart of Jesus. Thank You for the ways You use friendship to strengthen us and remind us that we are never alone.

Amen.

Think about the friends who have had the greatest impact on your faith journey. Write down the names of two or three friends who have been a source of encouragement for you. Take some time to pray for them this week, asking God to bless them and continue to strengthen your friendship.

If you feel led, reach out to one of those friends and thank them for the role they have played in your life. Let them know how much their friendship means to you and how God has used them to encourage you.

*Also, reflect on **Proverbs 17:17** and think about how you can be a friend who loves at all times, even in seasons of adversity.*

Chapter 6

TRUSTING GOD IN TOUGH TIMES

One of the hardest lessons I have learned in my journey of faith is that life does not always go the way we plan. There are times when we face difficulties so overwhelming that trusting God feels almost impossible. But it is in those moments, when we feel weakest and most helpless, that God shows us His strength.

My journey was filled with moments of joy and excitement, but it was also marked by seasons of deep pain and hardship. One of those seasons came when I faced the devastating loss of my brother and my mother. Those losses rocked me to my core, shaking the very foundation of my faith.

I remember the day I got the news about my brother. It was a phone call that changed my life. He had been in a tragic accident, and just like that, he was gone. My older brother had always been more than just a sibling—he was my best friend. We had grown up together, shared dreams and laughter, and had always supported each other. His sudden death left a hole in my heart that I did not know how to fill.

I cried out to God, asking why this had happened. I could not understand why God would take someone so close to me, someone so young. The grief was overwhelming, and for a while, it felt like my faith was unraveling. I had always trusted that God had a plan, but in that moment, I could not see it. All I could see was the pain.

A few years later, I was faced with another heartbreaking loss. My mother, who had always been my rock and my greatest supporter, was diagnosed with cancer. I prayed fervently for her healing, believing that God would answer my prayers. But as the months went by, her condition worsened. Watching her suffer was one of the hardest things I have ever experienced. I felt powerless, unable to do anything but pray and hope.

When she passed away, I was devastated. Losing my brother had been hard enough, but now my mother was gone too. I found myself questioning everything. Why would God allow this? Why had my prayers gone unanswered?

It was during that time of deep grief that I began to understand what it truly means to trust God. Trusting God does not mean that everything will be easy or that we will always get the answers we want. It means believing that God is good, even when life is not. It means knowing that He is with us, even when we feel completely alone.

In the midst of my grief, I turned to the Psalms, particularly **Psalm 34:18**, which says, "The Lord is close to the brokenhearted and saves those who are crushed in spirit." I clung to that promise, believing that even in my darkest moments, God was close to me. I did not have all the answers, but I knew that God had not abandoned me.

Slowly, God began to heal my heart. The pain did not go away overnight, but as I continued to pray and seek Him, I felt His presence in a way I never had before. God gave me the strength to keep going, to trust Him even when I could not see the whole picture.

Over time, I came to realize that trusting God is not about understanding everything. It is about surrendering our need for control and allowing

God to carry us through the storm. It is about believing that He is working all things for good, even when we cannot see how.

Looking back now, I see how God used those painful seasons to grow my faith. He did not remove the hardship, but He walked with me through it. And in that, I learned that God's faithfulness is greater than any pain we may face.

Reflection Verse

"The Lord is close to the brokenhearted and saves those who are crushed in spirit."

*— **Psalm 34:18 (NIV)***

Reflection

Life is full of ups and downs, and there will be times when you face hardships that feel too heavy to bear. In those moments, it can be tempting to doubt God's goodness or to wonder why He has allowed such pain in your life. But the Bible reminds us that God is close to the brokenhearted. He does not abandon us in our pain—He walks with us through it.

Have you ever faced a season of hardship? Maybe you've lost someone you love, or you have gone through something that made you question God's plan. Take a moment to reflect on how God was with you during that time, even when you could not see it. Trusting God does not mean having all the answers; it means believing that He is good, even when life is hard.

Prayer

Dear God,

Thank You for being with me in the tough times, even when I do not understand why things are happening. Help me to trust You more, even when I cannot see the bigger picture. Give me the strength to hold on to Your promises when life feels overwhelming and remind me that You are always close to me, especially when my heart is broken. Thank You for being my refuge and my strength.

Amen.

Think about a time in your life when you went through a tricky situation. It could be the loss of a loved one, a struggle with school or relationships, or a time when you felt like everything was falling apart. Write about how that experience made you feel and how you see God's presence in it now. If you are still going through it, take a moment to pray and ask God to help you trust Him in the middle of the storm.

Also, memorize **Psalm 34:18** *and let it be a reminder that God is always near, especially when you are hurting.*

Chapter 7

ADVENTURES IN GOD'S MISSION

When I first became a missionary, I had no idea just how much of an adventure it would be. I had grown up hearing about missionaries who traveled to far-off lands, risking their lives to share the Gospel with people who had never heard of Jesus. Their stories sounded exciting, but I never imagined that one day I would be part of such adventures.

After serving in my home country of Guyana, God began to open doors for me to go beyond what I had ever imagined. I knew He was calling me to Albania—a country that had been through years of political turmoil and was only just beginning to rebuild itself. It was a place that had been cut off from the outside world for so long, where religion had been banned, and where many people were just beginning to hear about Jesus for the first time.

The thought of going to Albania filled me with a mix of excitement and fear. I had never been to Europe before, and I knew nothing about the language or the culture. But deep down, I knew that this was where God was leading me. So, with my bags packed and a heart full of faith, I set off on a journey that would change my life forever.

Arriving in Albania was like stepping into a different world. The streets were lined with old, crumbling buildings that bore the marks of a country that had been through decades of communist rule. The people were warm and friendly, but there was also a sense of heaviness in the air, a reminder of the difficult past they had endured.

My first few weeks in Albania were a whirlwind of new experiences. I quickly realized that being a missionary was not just about preaching from a pulpit or handing out Bibles—it was about building relationships, understanding the culture, and earning the trust of the people. There were moments when I felt completely out of my depth, like when I had to navigate conversations in a language I barely understood or when I found myself in remote villages where the way of life was so different from anything I had ever known.

But amidst the challenges, there were moments of pure joy and wonder. One of the most unforgettable experiences came when I was invited to visit a small village high up in the mountains. The journey there was an adventure in itself. We traveled by jeep, bouncing along rocky, unpaved roads that wound their way through steep hills and dense forests. The further we went, the more remote and isolated the landscape became.

When we finally arrived, we were greeted by a group of villagers who welcomed us with open arms. They had never met a foreigner before, and they were eager to hear about the message we had come to share. We spent the afternoon sitting in a small, humble home, drinking tea, and talking about life and faith. As we spoke, I could see the curiosity in their eyes, the hunger to know more about the God we were talking about.

That evening, as the sun began to set over the mountains, we gathered in the village square for a time of prayer and worship. It was a simple, unplanned moment, but it became one of the most powerful experiences of my life. As we sang and prayed together, I could feel the presence of

God in a way I had not felt before. It was as if the mountains themselves were echoing our praise, and for a moment, I was overwhelmed by the beauty of what God was doing in that remote village.

I left that village with a renewed sense of purpose. I realized that the adventure of following God was not just about the places we go—it was about the people we meet along the way. Every conversation, every relationship, every act of love was part of the bigger story God was writing. And in those moments, I saw the sincere heart of missions—not just as a task to be completed, but as an opportunity to be part of God's incredible plan to reach the world.

But the adventure did not stop there. My time in Albania was filled with moments that tested my faith and pushed me to rely on God in ways I never had before. There were days when I felt completely overwhelmed by the challenges of ministry. The language barrier was difficult to overcome, and there were moments when I felt like I was not making any impact at all.

One of the most challenging times came when I was invited to lead a youth camp in a remote area. It was supposed to be a week of fun activities, Bible lessons, and fellowship with young people from across the region. But as the week began, everything seemed to go wrong. The weather turned cold and rainy, making it impossible to do many of the outdoor activities we had planned. The young people, who had come expecting a week of adventure, quickly became restless and frustrated.

I remember sitting in my room one night, feeling completely defeated. I had no idea how to turn things around. I prayed, asking God to give me wisdom and guidance, but I felt like I was at the end of my rope.

Then, in the middle of the night, I had an idea. What if, instead of focusing on the activities we could not do, we focused on the ones we could? I gathered the team the next morning and shared my thoughts.

We decided to scrap the original schedule and instead focus on building deeper connections with the young people through small group discussions, prayer times, and personal testimonies.

What happened next was nothing short of miraculous. The young people, who had been disappointed and frustrated, began to open in ways I had not expected. They shared their struggles, their fears, and their hopes for the future. We prayed together, laughed together, and by the end of the week, something had shifted. The camp that had seemed like a failure at the beginning had become a powerful time of transformation for everyone involved, including me.

That experience taught me a valuable lesson: the adventure of following God is not always about things going according to plan. It is about being willing to adapt, to trust that God is in control, and to see every challenge as an opportunity for Him to work in ways we cannot even imagine.

As I look back on my time in Albania, I see how God used those experiences to shape me, not just as a missionary, but as a follower of Jesus. The adventure of God's mission is unpredictable, full of surprises, and often takes us out of our comfort zones. But it is also where we see God's power and love most clearly. Whether it is in a remote village in the mountains or in the everyday moments of ministry, God is always at work, inviting us to join Him in His incredible adventure.

Reflection Verse

"Therefore, go and make disciples of all nations, baptizing them in the name of the Father and of the Son and of the Holy Spirit."

— Matthew 28:19 (NIV)

Reflection

Have you ever thought about what it means to be on an adventure with God? Sometimes we think that following God is all about playing it safe, but the truth is, God often calls us to step out into the unknown. It might be sharing your faith with someone new, taking on a challenge that feels impossible, or going somewhere that takes you out of your comfort zone.

What adventure is God calling you to? Maybe it's something small, like talking to a friend about your faith, or maybe it is something big, like going on a mission trip or serving in a new way. Whatever it is, remember that God is with you every step of the way, guiding you, and working through you in ways you cannot even imagine.

Prayer

Dear God,

Thank You for inviting me to be part of Your mission. Help me to trust You as I step out in faith, even when I do not know what lies ahead. Give me the courage to follow where You lead, and remind me that You are always with me, no matter how challenging the journey may be. Thank You for the adventure of following You, and for the opportunity to be part of Your incredible plan to reach the world. Amen.

Think about the last time you stepped out of your comfort zone for God. Maybe it was sharing your faith with someone, taking on a new challenge, or going on a mission trip. How did that experience shape you? Write about it in your journal, and reflect on how God worked through that situation, even if it did not go as planned.

If you have not had an experience like that yet, take some time to pray and ask God what adventure He is calling you to. It might be something small or something big, but whatever it is, trust that God will guide you and use you in ways you never imagined.

*Also, read **Matthew 28:19** and imagine yourself being part of the Great Commission—going out into the world to make disciples. How does that inspire you to live boldly for God?*

Chapter 8

LEARNING TO FORGIVE

Forgiveness is one of the hardest things we are called to do as Christians. It is easy to talk about forgiveness when everything is going well, but when someone has hurt us deeply, forgiveness feels like an impossible task. Yet, it is one of the most powerful acts of love and obedience to God that we can offer.

My journey with forgiveness started in a place I never expected—on the mission field. I thought that being a missionary was all about sharing God's love and helping others, and it is. But what I did not realize was that God was also going to use the mission field to teach me some of the hardest lessons of my life, and one of those lessons was about forgiveness.

During my time in Albania, I was working with a fellow missionary, someone I trusted and considered a close friend. We had been through a lot together, and I thought we were on the same page, working toward the same goal of sharing the Gospel and helping people grow in their faith. But slowly, I began to notice that things were not right. This friend started distancing themselves from me, becoming more secretive about their plans and actions.

At first, I tried to brush it off. Maybe they were just going through something personal, I thought. But as time went on, the situation got worse. I found out that this person had been talking behind my back, spreading rumors, and undermining the work we had done together. Worse still, they had been trying to take control of the ministry we had built, turning people against me in the process.

When I discovered the full extent of what was happening, I was devastated. This was not just a betrayal of trust—it felt like a personal attack on everything I had worked so hard for. I was angry, hurt, and confused. How could someone I had trusted so much do something like this? How could someone who claimed to follow Jesus' act in such a way?

In the days that followed, I wrestled with my emotions. I wanted to confront this person, to let them know how much they had hurt me. I wanted justice, for the truth to come out and for them to face the consequences of their actions. But as I prayed about it, God began to speak to my heart in a way that was both challenging and convicting.

Jesus taught His followers to forgive, not just once or twice, but over and over again. In **Matthew 18:21-22**, Peter asked Jesus how many times he should forgive someone who sins against him, suggesting seven times might be enough. But Jesus replied, "I tell you, not seven times, but seventy-seven times." That answer shook me. Jesus was not just asking us to forgive a set number of times—He was calling us to live a life marked by forgiveness, to be willing to forgive as often as it was needed, just as He forgives us.

But how could I forgive someone who had hurt me so deeply? How could I let go of the anger and bitterness that had taken root in my heart? Every time I thought about what had happened, I felt that familiar surge of anger rise up again.

That is when I realized something important: forgiveness is not about forgetting the hurt or pretending it did not happen. It is about releasing the burden of bitterness and trusting God to handle the situation. It is about choosing to love, even when love feels impossible. Jesus did not ask us to forgive because it is easy—He asked us to forgive because it sets us free.

I knew I could not do it on my own. I needed God's help. So, I began to pray, not just for my own healing, but for the person who had wronged me. At first, the prayers felt forced. I did not want to pray for them. I did not want to ask God to bless them. But as I continued to pray, something began to change in my heart. Slowly, I felt the grip of anger loosen. The more I prayed, the more God softened my heart, and I began to see this person through His eyes—as someone who, like me, was flawed and in need of grace.

It did not happen overnight, but over time, I was able to forgive. It did not mean I forgot what had happened or that everything went back to the way it was before. But I no longer carried the burden of anger and resentment. I had given it to God, trusting Him to bring healing and justice in His time.

Forgiveness is powerful. It sets us free from the chains of bitterness that keep us bound. It allows us to live in the fullness of God's grace, knowing that just as we have been forgiven, we are called to forgive others.

One of the greatest examples of forgiveness is Jesus Himself. As He hung on the cross, enduring unimaginable pain and suffering, He looked down at the people who had betrayed Him, mocked Him, and nailed Him to the cross, and He prayed, "Father, forgive them, for they do not know what they are doing" (Luke 23:34). In that moment, Jesus showed us the depth of God's love and the power of forgiveness.

If Jesus could forgive those who crucified Him, how much more should we be willing to forgive those who wrong us? Forgiveness is not just something we do for others—it is something we do for ourselves. It releases us from the burden of bitterness and allows God's love to flow freely in our hearts.

Reflection Verse

"Be kind and compassionate to one another, forgiving each other, just as in Christ God forgave you."

*— **Ephesians 4:32 (NIV)***

Reflection

Forgiving someone who has hurt you is never easy. It can feel like an impossible task, especially when the pain runs deep. But the Bible reminds us that we are called to forgive, just as God has forgiven us. Forgiveness does not mean pretending the hurt never happened—it means choosing to release the bitterness and trust God to bring healing.

Is there someone in your life you need to forgive? Maybe it's a friend who betrayed you, a family member who hurt you, or even yourself. Take some time to pray and ask God to help you forgive, even when it feels impossible. Remember, forgiveness sets you free.

Prayer

Dear God,

Thank You for showing me what true forgiveness looks like. Help me to forgive those who have hurt me, even when it feels hard. I know that holding on to anger and bitterness only hurts me, and I want to live in the freedom that comes from forgiving.

Give me the strength to release my hurt into Your hands and trust that You will bring healing in Your time. Thank You for forgiving me and help me to show that same grace to others.

Amen.

Think of someone who has hurt you in the past. It could be a friend, a family member, or even yourself. Take some time to write down how that experience made you feel. Then, ask God to help you forgive that person. If you feel ready, write a prayer of forgiveness, asking God to release the hurt and bitterness from your heart.

Also, read **Ephesians 4:32** *and reflect on what it means to forgive as Christ forgave you. How can you show kindness and compassion to others, even when they do not deserve it?*

Chapter 9

GOD'S PLAN IS ALWAYS GOOD

It is often said that God has a plan for our lives, and most of the time, that is comforting to hear. But what happens when life does not go the way we expect? When things fall apart and our dreams seem out of reach, it can be difficult to trust that God's plan is still good.

In my journey, I have faced many moments where I questioned God's plan for my life. I could not see how the struggles, setbacks, and disappointments fit into His good plan. But over time, I have come to understand that God's plan does not always look like what we expect, and yet, it is always good.

One of the most profound lessons I learned about trusting God's plan came when I was serving in Albania. I had been in the country for a few years, and we had built a small but growing ministry. We were working with young people, sharing the Gospel, and seeing lives changed. I was passionate about the work and excited to see what God was doing.

But then, out of nowhere, things began to unravel. Several key members of our team left, leaving us short-handed and struggling to keep the ministry going. At the same time, funding became a significant issue, and we had to cut back on many of the programs we had worked so hard to build. It felt like everything I had poured my heart into was falling apart.

I remember sitting in my small apartment one night, overwhelmed by the weight of it all. I had come to Albania believing that God had called me there for a purpose, but now I was not so sure. Why would God allow things to fall apart like this? Had I misunderstood His plan for me? Was I doing something wrong?

As I sat in the quiet, I opened my Bible to **Romans 8:28**, a verse I had read many times before: "And we know that in all things God works for the good of those who love him, who have been called according to his purpose." I had always found comfort in that verse, but in that moment, it felt distant. How could God be working for my good when everything around me was crumbling?

I prayed, asking God to help me understand. I did not get an immediate answer, but over the next few weeks, God began to show me something important: His plan is not always about success in the way we define it. Sometimes, God allows things to fall apart so that something better can take shape. He was not asking me to understand everything—He was asking me to trust that He was still in control, even when it did not feel like it.

As the months went by, I started to see God's hand in the midst of the challenges. New opportunities began to open up—opportunities I never would have considered if things had continued the way they were. We started partnering with other ministries, which brought fresh energy and new vision to the work we were doing. I met people who became instrumental in helping us rebuild, and slowly but surely, the ministry began to grow again.

Looking back now, I see that God's plan was always good. Even though I could not see it at the time, He was working behind the scenes, preparing the way for something better than I had imagined. It was not the plan I would have chosen, but it was the plan that ultimately brought more growth, more impact, and more opportunities to share the Gospel.

That experience taught me something crucial: God's plan does not always follow our timeline, and it does not always look the way we expect it to. But His plan is always good, and He is always working for our good, even in the hardest moments.

There were other times in my life when I questioned God's plan—when I faced personal struggles, loss, and disappointment. One of the hardest seasons came when I lost my mother and brother. I could not understand why God would allow such painful losses to happen. I prayed for healing, I prayed for miracles, but they did not come in the way I had hoped.

In those moments of grief, I had to hold on to the truth that God's plan is good, even when I cannot see it. **Jeremiah 29:11** reminds us of God's promise: "For I know the plans I have for you, declares the Lord, plans to prosper you and not to harm you, plans to give you hope and a future." It is a verse I turned to many times, not because it erased the pain, but because it reminded me that God was still with me, guiding my steps, even though the darkest valleys.

As I journeyed through those difficult seasons, I began to see how God was using those experiences to shape me, to deepen my faith, and to prepare me for the next steps in His plan. The loss of my family members left a void in my life, but it also opened doors for me to connect with others who had experienced similar grief. I was able to share my story with people who were struggling, and in doing so, I saw how God was using my pain to bring comfort and hope to others.

God's plan is bigger than we can imagine. He sees the whole picture, while we only see a part of it. And while we may not always understand why certain things happen, we can trust that He is working for our good, even in the midst of the hardest trials.

One of the most beautiful examples of this truth is found in the story of Joseph in the Bible. Joseph's life was full of ups and downs—betrayed by his brothers, sold into slavery, falsely accused, and imprisoned. But through it all, God had a plan. In the end, Joseph was elevated to a position of power, where he was able to save his family and an entire nation from famine. In **Genesis 50:20,** Joseph said to his brothers, "You intended to harm me, but God intended it for good to accomplish what is now being done, the saving of many lives."

Joseph's story is a powerful reminder that God can take even the most painful circumstances and use them for His glory and our good. It does not mean that the pain is not real or that the struggles are not hard. But it does mean that God is always at work, weaving every part of our lives into His greater plan.

Reflection Verse

"And we know that in all things God works for the good of those who love him, who have been called according to his purpose."

*— **Romans 8:28 (NIV)***

Reflection

Trusting God's plan is not always easy, especially when life does not go the way we expect. But the Bible reminds us that God is always working for our good, even in the hardest times. We may not understand why certain things happen, but we can trust that God sees the bigger picture and that His plan is always good.

Think about a time in your life when things did not go the way you expected. How did it make you feel? Looking back now, can you see how God was working in that situation, even if it did not make sense at the time?

Prayer

Dear God,

Thank You for reminding me that Your plan is always good, even when I cannot see it. Help me to trust You in the hard times, to believe that You are working for my good, even when things do not go the way I expect. Give me the strength to hold on to Your promises, knowing that You are in control and that Your plan is better than anything I could imagine. Thank You for being with me in every season of life, and for guiding my steps according to Your good purpose. Amen.

Take a moment to reflect on a time when you struggled to trust God's plan. Write about that experience in a journal and think about how God has worked in your life since then. If you are still going through a difficult season, spend some time in prayer, asking God to help you trust Him, even when you do not understand what He is doing.

Also, memorize **Romans 8:28** *and keep it close to your heart, reminding yourself that God is always working for your good, even when life is hard.*

Chapter 10

COURAGE TO KEEP GOING

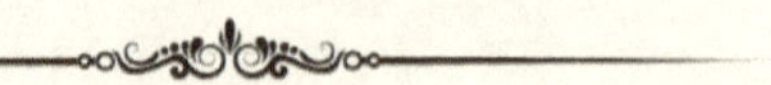

Perseverance in faith is one of the most important lessons we can learn. Following Jesus is not always easy—there are moments when it feels like the challenges are too big, the road is too hard, and we just do not have the strength to keep going. But it is in those moments, when we want to give up, that God calls us to find courage in Him and keep pressing forward.

I have had many moments in my life when I wanted to quit. The journey of faith is full of obstacles, and there have been times when the weight of it all felt overwhelming. But time and time again, God has shown me that He gives us the strength to keep going, even when we think we have reached our limit.

One of the hardest seasons I faced was during my ministry in Albania. We were working hard to build relationships, share the Gospel, and serve the community. At first, things seemed to be going well—we saw young people coming to faith, and we were starting to make an impact. But then, seemingly out of nowhere, everything became difficult. People who had been interested in learning about Jesus stopped coming to meetings, funding for our programs began to dry up, and some of the team members I was working with decided to leave.

I felt like everything I had worked for was falling apart. I had come to Albania with a heart full of hope, ready to serve and make a difference, but now it seemed like all my efforts were in vain. I remember sitting alone one evening, completely discouraged, wondering if I had misunderstood God's calling. Was I supposed to be here? Had I failed?

As I sat there, feeling the weight of my discouragement, I prayed. I did not have the words to express what I was feeling, but I knew I needed God's help. In that moment, a verse from **Isaiah 40:31** came to mind: "But those who hope in the Lord will renew their strength. They will soar on wings like eagles; they will run and not grow weary; they will walk and not be faint."

That verse was like a lifeline. I realized that I had been relying on my own strength, trying to carry the weight of the ministry on my own shoulders. But God was reminding me that true strength comes from Him. He was not asking me to carry the burden alone—He was asking me to trust Him, to lean on Him for the strength I needed to keep going.

In the days that followed, I began to change my perspective. Instead of focusing on what was not working, I started to look for the small ways God was still moving. I saw His hand in the relationships we had built, in the seeds that had been planted, even if we were not seeing immediate results. And little by little, my strength was renewed.

The challenges did not disappear overnight. There were still hard days, still moments of doubt. But I found courage in knowing that God was with me, that He had called me to this place for a purpose, and that He would give me the strength to see it through.

This was not the only time I needed to find courage to keep going. Later in my journey, when I moved to Finland, I faced similar challenges. Learning a new language, adapting to a new culture, and building relationships in a place where Christianity was not always well understood—it all took a toll on me. There were times when I felt isolated and wondered if I was making any difference at all.

But once again, God reminded me that He is the source of my strength. Through prayer, through the encouragement of friends, and through the promises of Scripture, I found the courage to keep moving forward, even when the path seemed difficult.

What I have learned is this: courage does not mean we never feel afraid or discouraged. Courage means we keep going, even when we are scared. It means trusting that God is with us, that He sees the bigger picture, and that He will give us the strength we need to face whatever comes our way.

One of the stories in the Bible that has always inspired me is the story of Joshua. After Moses died, Joshua was called to lead the Israelites into the Promised Land—a daunting task, to say the least. In **Joshua 1:9**, God says to him, "Have I not commanded you? Be strong and courageous. Do not be afraid; do not be discouraged, for the Lord your God will be with you wherever you go."

That verse is a powerful reminder that courage is not about our own strength—it is about trusting in God's presence. Joshua faced incredible challenges, but God was with him every step of the way. And that same God is with us, calling us to be strong and courageous in the face of our own battles.

Whatever challenges you are facing, remember this: God is with you. You do not have to carry the burden alone. When you feel like you cannot take another step, ask God for strength. When you feel discouraged, turn to Him in prayer and let Him renew your spirit. He has promised to never leave you or forsake you, and He will give you the courage you need to keep going.

Reflection Verse

"But those who hope in the Lord will renew their strength. They will soar on wings like eagles; they will run and not grow weary; they will walk and not be faint."

— Isaiah 40:31 (NIV)

Reflection

Have you ever faced a time when you felt like giving up? Maybe it was because of a difficult situation at school, a challenge in your relationships, or a struggle in your faith. It is normal to feel discouraged at times, but the Bible reminds us that God is our source of strength. When we put our hope in Him, He renews our strength and gives us the courage to keep going.

Think about a time when you felt like giving up. How did you find the strength to keep going? If you are going through a tough time now, take a moment to pray and ask God for the courage you need to keep moving forward.

Prayer

Dear God,

Thank You for being my source of strength when I feel weak. Help me to trust You in the difficult times and remind me that I do not have to carry the burden alone. When I feel like giving up, give me the courage to keep going, knowing that You are with me every step of the way. Thank You for the promise that You will never leave me or forsake me, and for the strength You provide when I put my hope in You. Amen.

Think about something in your life right now that feels challenging—whether it is a relationship, a difficult situation at school, or a personal struggle. Write it down in a journal and take a moment to pray, asking God to give you the strength and courage to keep going. Trust that He is with you, even when things feel hard.

Also, memorize **Isaiah 40:31** *and let it be a reminder that when you hope in the Lord, He will renew your strength. Whenever you feel discouraged, repeat that verse to yourself and remember that God is always with you.*

Chapter 11

SHARING GOD'S LOVE

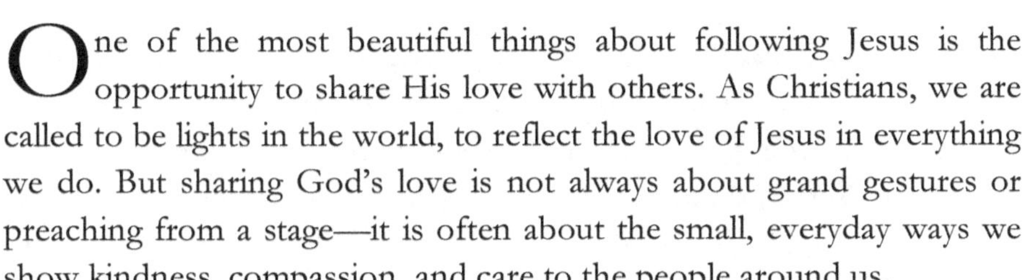

One of the most beautiful things about following Jesus is the opportunity to share His love with others. As Christians, we are called to be lights in the world, to reflect the love of Jesus in everything we do. But sharing God's love is not always about grand gestures or preaching from a stage—it is often about the small, everyday ways we show kindness, compassion, and care to the people around us.

When I first became a missionary, I thought that sharing God's love meant doing something big—like traveling to far-off places or preaching to crowds of people. And while there have been moments in my life where I have had the chance to do those things, I have learned that sharing God's love happens in so many different ways, both big and small.

One of the most powerful lessons I learned about sharing God's love came during my time in Albania. I was working in a community where many people had never heard the Gospel before, and I knew that part of my mission was to tell them about Jesus. But what I did not realize at first was how important it was to show them God's love through my actions, not just my words.

There was a young man in the community who had grown up in a difficult environment. He had faced a lot of hardship in his life, and as a result, he was skeptical of anything to do with faith or religion. He kept his distance from the church and from any kind of spiritual conversation, and at first, I was not sure how to reach him.

But as time went on, I began to build a relationship with him. I did not try to preach to him or force him to listen to a message. Instead, I spent time with him, listened to his stories, and helped him with whatever he needed. Sometimes, it was as simple as sitting with him during a tough day or offering to pray for him when he felt overwhelmed. Little by little, he began to open up, and eventually, he started asking questions about God and faith.

One day, he told me that what had impacted him most was not the words I had said—it was the way I had treated him. He saw something different in the way I lived, in the way I showed kindness and care, and that is what drew him to ask more about Jesus. It was a reminder to me that sharing God's love is not just about what we say—it is about how we live.

There have been so many moments like that throughout my journey as a missionary. Whether it is helping someone who is struggling, offering a listening ear, or simply being present with people in their time of need, I have seen how God's love can shine through in the most ordinary ways. And every time I see someone's life touched by that love, I am reminded of how powerful it is.

But sharing God's love is not limited to the mission field. We are called to share His love wherever we are—at school, at work, in our families, and with our friends. Sometimes, it is the smallest acts of kindness that make the biggest difference. A smile, a kind word, a helping hand—these are all ways we can reflect God's love in our daily lives.

In **Matthew 5:14-16**, Jesus says, "You are the light of the world. A town built on a hill cannot be hidden. Neither do people light a lamp and put it under a bowl. Instead, they put it on its stand, and it gives light to everyone in the house. In the same way, let your light shine before others, that they may see your good deeds and glorify your Father in heaven."

I love that image of being a light in the world. A light does not need to shout or draw attention to itself—it simply shines, illuminating the darkness around it. In the same way, when we live out our faith through acts of love and kindness, we become a light to those around us, pointing them to Jesus.

But sharing God's love also requires courage. There will be times when it is not easy, when we feel nervous or afraid to talk about our faith. I remember a time when in Finland, and I had become friends with a young man who did not know much about Christianity. He was curious about my faith, but he did not come from a religious background, and I could tell he had a lot of questions.

One evening, we were sitting together after a long day, and he started asking me about why I believed in Jesus. I could tell that this was an important moment, but I also felt nervous. What if I said the wrong thing? What if I could not explain it well enough? What if he did not understand?

But then I remembered something: sharing God's love is not about having all the right answers. It is about being honest, being kind, and trusting that God will work through the conversation. So, I shared my story. I told him about how Jesus had changed my life, how I had experienced God's love and grace in ways I never could have imagined. I did not have all the answers to his questions, but I shared from my heart.

To my surprise, that conversation opened the door for many more. Over time, he became more and more interested in learning about Jesus, and eventually, he made the decision to follow Christ. That experience taught me that sharing God's love is not about being perfect—it is about being willing. God can work through our words and actions, even when we feel inadequate.

Wherever you are in life, God has given you opportunities to share His love with the people around you. It does not have to be complicated. Sometimes, it is as simple as being a good friend, offering to pray for someone, or showing kindness in a difficult situation. Every act of love, no matter how small, reflects the heart of Jesus to the world.

One of the most powerful ways we can share God's love is by living out the commandment Jesus gave us in **John 13:34-35**: "A new command I give you: Love one another. As I have loved you, so you must love one another. By this, everyone will know that you are my disciples, if you love one another."

That is what sets us apart as followers of Jesus—our love for one another. When people see the way we love, they see a glimpse of who Jesus is. It is not always easy to love, especially when people hurt us or when we are tired and overwhelmed. But Jesus calls us to love anyway, to show His grace and compassion to everyone we meet.

Reflection Verse

"A new command I give you: Love one another. As I have loved you, so you must love one another. By this, everyone will know that you are my disciples, if you love one another."

— John 13:34-35 (NIV)

Reflection

Sharing God's love does not have to be complicated. Sometimes, it is the small acts of kindness and care that make the biggest difference. Think about the people in your life—your family, friends, classmates, or neighbors. How can you show God's love to them? Maybe it's by being a good listener, offering to help with something, or simply being there when they need you. Every act of love points people to Jesus.

Who in your life needs to experience God's love right now? Take a moment to pray for them and ask God to show you how you can be a light in their life.

Prayer

Dear God,

Thank You for the opportunity to share Your love with others. Help me to be a light in the world, showing kindness, compassion, and care to the people around me. Give me the courage to share my faith, even when I feel nervous, and remind me that You can work through my words and actions, no matter how small they may seem. Help me to love others the way You love me, and let my life be a reflection of Your grace and goodness.

Amen.

Activity

Think about someone in your life who could use some encouragement or kindness this week. It could be a friend, a family member, or someone you do not know very well. Write down a few ways you can show God's love to them—whether it is through a kind word, a thoughtful gesture, or simply spending time with them. Then, make a plan to put it into action.

*Also, memorize **John 13:34-35**, and let it remind you that loving others is one of the most powerful ways to share your faith.*

Chapter 12

LIVING FOR GOD EVERY DAY

One of the most important lessons I have learned on my journey of faith is that living for God is not just about the big moments or the extraordinary events—it is about how we live every single day. Being a follower of Jesus means that our faith should impact every area of our lives, from the way we treat others to the choices we make when no one is watching. It is not just about going to church or reading the Bible—it is about letting God guide our thoughts, our actions, and our words in everything we do.

When I first became a missionary, I had this idea that living for God meant doing things that were obviously spiritual—like preaching, praying, or leading Bible studies. And while those things are incredibly important, what I have come to realize is that the way we live for God in the everyday moments matters just as much.

I learned this lesson in an unexpected way during my time in Albania. I was busy with the ministry, meeting new people, sharing the Gospel, and building relationships in the community. Every day seemed full of opportunities to serve God and share His love. But after a few months, I started to feel overwhelmed. The constant activity left me exhausted, and I began to question whether I was truly living for God or just going through the motions.

One evening, after a particularly long day, I decided to take a walk to clear my head. As I walked through the streets of the town, I saw a man sitting alone on a bench. He looked tired and a little sad. Something in my heart told me to stop and talk to him, but I hesitated. I was tired, and I was not sure I had the energy for another conversation.

But then I remembered something a mentor once told me: "Living for God isn't about doing something big every time—it's about being faithful in the small things." So, I stopped, sat down next to the man, and asked him how he was doing.

We talked for a while, and it became clear that he was going through a hard time. He had lost his job, and his family was struggling. He did not know what to do, and he felt like giving up. I listened as he shared his story, and then I offered to pray for him. It was not a big, dramatic moment, but it was a moment of connection—one that reminded me that living for God often happens in the small, everyday moments when we take time to care for someone else.

As I walked back to my apartment that night, I realized that living for God does not always look like preaching to crowds or going on mission trips. Sometimes, it looks like sitting with someone who is hurting, listening to their story, and reminding them that they are not alone. It is about being faithful in the little things—showing kindness, offering a helping hand, and living in a way that reflects God's love in everything we do.

One of the verses that has always inspired me is **Colossians 3:17**, which says, "And whatever you do, whether in word or deed, do it all in the name of the Lord Jesus, giving thanks to God the Father through Him." That verse challenges me to think about how I live my life on a daily basis. It is a reminder that every word I speak, every action I take, can be done as an act of worship to God.

Living for God every day is not about being perfect—it is about being intentional. It is about waking up each morning and asking God to guide your steps, to help you see the opportunities around you to share His love, and to live in a way that honors Him. It is about choosing to do the right thing, even when it is hard. It is about being kind when you do not feel like it, forgiving when you would rather hold a grudge, and trusting God's plan even when it does not make sense.

There were times in my journey when I struggled to live for God in the trivial things. I remember a season when I was working long hours, trying to juggle the demands of ministry and everyday life. I was tired, frustrated, and honestly, I just wanted a break. I found myself getting impatient with the people around me, snapping at my friends, and losing sight of why I was there in the first place.

One day, after a particularly hard conversation with a friend, I sat down and prayed, asking God to help me refocus. In that moment, I felt Him reminding me that living for Him is not just about the big ministry moments—it is about how I treat the people He has placed in my life every day. It is about being kind when I am tired, being patient when I am frustrated, and loving others even when I do not feel like it.

That was a turning point for me. I realized that living for God every day means paying attention to the trivial things—the way I talk to people, the choices I make when no one is looking, and the way I respond when life does not go the way I expect. It is in those small, everyday moments that our faith is truly tested.

One of the greatest examples of this is Jesus Himself. Throughout the Gospels, we see Jesus living for God in both the big and small moments. He preached to crowds, performed miracles, and changed lives in extraordinary ways. But He also took time for the small, everyday acts of love and kindness. He noticed the people others overlooked. He took time to pray, to rest, and to care for those in need. And through it all, He lived every moment in obedience to God's will.

In **Matthew 25:40,** Jesus says, "Truly I tell you, whatever you did for one of the least of these brothers and sisters of mine, you did for me." That verse reminds us that living for God means loving and serving others, especially those who are in need. It is not always about doing something grand—it is about being faithful in the small, everyday acts of kindness that reflect God's heart.

Wherever you are in life, whether you are in school, working, or spending time with family and friends, you have the opportunity to live for God every day. It is not about being perfect—it is about being willing to let God guide your steps, to love others, and to be a reflection of His grace in everything you do.

Reflection Verse

"And whatever you do, whether in word or deed, do it all in the name of the Lord Jesus, giving thanks to God the Father through Him."— **Colossians 3:17 (NIV)**

Reflection

Living for God every day does not have to be complicated. It is about choosing to honor Him in the small moments—the way we talk, the way we act, and the way we treat others. Think about your daily life—how can you live for God in the ordinary moments? Maybe it's by being kind to a classmate who is having a hard day, or by choosing to forgive someone who has hurt you. Every small act of faithfulness matters to God.

Take a moment to reflect on how you can live for God in your daily life. What changes can you make to ensure that your words and actions reflect His love and grace?

Prayer

Dear God,

Thank You for reminding me that living for You is not just about the big moments—it is about how I live every day. Help me to be faithful in the small things, to show kindness, love, and grace to the people around me. Guide my steps and my words, so that everything I do reflects Your heart. Give me the strength to live for You, even when it is hard, and help me to trust that You are with me in every moment.

Amen.

Activity

Think about one area of your life where you could be more intentional about living for God. Maybe it's the way you talk to your family, the way you treat your friends, or the choices you make when you are alone. Write down a few practical steps you can take to live for God in that area and pray for His guidance as you make those changes.

Also, memorize **Colossians 3:17** *and let it remind you that every word and action can be an act of worship when you do it for God.*

Chapter 13

KEEP WALKING WITH GOD

Life can feel like a series of steps—some small, some big, and some that lead us in directions we never expected. In my journey, I have learned that the most important thing we can do is keep walking with God, no matter where those steps take us. It is not always easy, and sometimes the path is unclear, but when we walk with God, He leads us to places we could never reach on our own.

When I was a young boy growing up in Guyana, I had no idea where my life would take me. I did not know that I had eventually become a missionary, travel to different countries, and have experiences that would shape my faith in ways I could not have imagined. But what I did know, even as a teenager, was that I wanted to follow God. I wanted my life to matter, and I wanted to do something meaningful for Him.

Looking back now, I see how every step I took—both the good ones and the hard ones—was part of a bigger journey that God was leading me on. And that journey is not over yet. I am still walking with God every day, learning new things, facing new challenges, and trusting that He has a plan for my life, just as He has a plan for yours.

One of the most important things I have learned is that walking with God does not mean everything will always go smoothly. There have been plenty of times in my life when I have faced difficulties—times when I felt lost, confused, or unsure of what to do next. I have gone through seasons of loss, disappointment, and uncertainty. But through it all I have learned to trust that God is with me, even when the path is difficult.

When I moved to Albania to serve as a missionary, I was full of excitement and hope. I knew that God had called me there, and I was ready to make a difference. But after a while, the challenges started to pile up. I faced opposition from people who did not understand why I was there. I struggled with the language barrier and the cultural differences. There were days when I felt isolated and discouraged, and I wondered if I had made a mistake.

But in those moments, God reminded me that walking with Him means trusting His plan, even when it does not make sense. I had to keep taking steps forward, even when I did not not know what the outcome would be. And as I kept walking, I began to see how God was working through every challenge, opening doors did not expect and bringing people into my life who needed to hear about His love.

It is easy to follow God when everything is going well, but the real test of faith comes when life gets hard. Will you keep walking with God when the path is steep? Will you trust Him when you do not know what is ahead?

One of the stories that has always inspired me is the story of Peter walking on water in **Matthew 14:28-31**. When the disciples saw Jesus' walking on the water toward them, Peter was the only one brave enough to ask, "Lord, if it's You, tell me to come to You on the water." Jesus told him to come, and Peter stepped out of the boat and began walking toward Him. But when Peter saw the wind and the waves, he became afraid and started to sink. Jesus reached out His hand and caught him, saying, "You of little faith, why did you doubt?"

That story reminds me that walking with God requires faith, especially when the "winds and waves" of life start to make us doubt. It is easy to focus on the things that scare us—the challenges, the unknowns, the fears. But when we keep our eyes on Jesus, we can walk through those storms with confidence, knowing that He is with us, ready to catch us when we stumble.

There have been times in my life when I have felt like Peter, taking bold steps of faith, only to be overwhelmed by fear and doubt. But every time I have felt myself start to sink, God has been there to lift me up, reminding me that I do not have to walk this journey alone. He is with me, guiding my steps, giving me strength, and showing me the way forward.

For young people like you, walking with God can feel both exciting and scary. Maybe you've felt God calling you to do something that seems big or intimidating, like sharing your faith with a friend or standing up for what is right when everyone around you is going in a different direction. Maybe you're unsure about the future and wondering how God's plan will unfold in your life. Whatever your journey looks like right now, I want to encourage you: keep walking with God.

It does not matter how young you are—God has a plan for your life. When I first felt God calling me, I was only 13 years old, and I had no idea what my future would look like. But as I have walked with God, He has opened doors, provided for me in ways I never imagined, and led me on adventures that have deepened my faith and helped me grow in ways I never could have on my own.

In **Proverbs 3:5-6**, the Bible says, "Trust in the Lord with all your heart and lean not on your own understanding; in all your ways submit to Him, and He will make your paths straight." That is a promise you can hold onto as you take each step of faith. You do not have to have all the answers. You do not have to know what the future holds. You just need to trust that God is guiding your steps, and He will make your path clear.

One of the things I have learned on my journey is that walking with God is not just about the destination it is about the process. Every step you take with Him is an opportunity to grow, to learn, and to experience His love in new ways. Even when the road is hard, and you feel like giving up, God is using those moments to shape you, to strengthen your faith, and to prepare you for what is next.

So how do we keep walking with God every day? It starts with spending time with Him. Reading the Bible, praying, and surrounding yourself with other believers who can encourage you are all ways to stay connected to God. But it also means making choices that reflect your faith—choosing to be kind when others are not, standing up for what is right, even when it is unpopular, and trusting God in the big and small moments of your life.

I want to challenge you to think about the steps you are taking in your life right now. Are you walking with God? Are you trusting Him, even when the road is difficult? Are you willing to step out in faith, even when you are unsure of what is ahead? My prayer for you is that you will keep walking with God, no matter where He leads you. Because when you walk with God there is no limit to what He can do through you.

Reflection Verse

"Trust in the Lord with all your heart and lean not on your own understanding; in all your ways submit to Him, and He will make your paths straight."

— Proverbs 3:5-6 (NIV)

Reflection

Walking with God means trusting Him in every step of your journey. Sometimes the road is clear, and other times, it is filled with challenges and uncertainties. But when you trust God, you can walk with confidence, knowing that He is guiding your path.

What steps of faith is God calling you to take right now? Are there areas in your life where you are struggling to trust Him? Take a moment to reflect on how you can keep walking with God, even when the road is hard.

Prayer

Dear God,

Thank You for walking with me through every step of my life. Help me to trust You, even when the path is difficult, and to keep my eyes on You when fear and doubt try to overwhelm me. Give me the courage to take bold steps of faith, knowing that You are always with me, guiding me and making my path straight. Help me to walk with You every day, trusting that Your plan for my life is good.

Amen.

Think about a time when you had to trust God, even when you did not know what would happen next. How did it feel to take that step of faith? Write about that experience in a journal and reflect on how God has been with you in every step of your journey.

*Also, memorize **Proverbs 3:5-6** and let it be a reminder to trust God with all your heart, knowing that He will guide your path.*

Chapter 14

EMBRACING THE ADVENTURE

Faith is more than a belief—it is an adventure. When you choose to follow God, you are signing up for a journey that will take you places you never imagined, challenge you in ways you never expected, and fill your life with purpose, excitement, and meaning. But like any adventure, there will be moments of joy and moments of struggle. The key is learning to embrace the adventure, trusting that God is with you every step of the way.

One of the things I have learned from my own journey is that when you follow God, there is never a dull moment. Growing up in Guyana, I had no idea that I would one day become a missionary and travel to places like Albania, Finland, and other parts of the world. I never imagined that I would have the chance to share the Gospel with people from diverse cultures, face the challenges of living in unfamiliar environments, or experience the incredible ways God would work through my life.

But that is the thing about following God—He leads us on adventures that are far beyond anything we could plan for ourselves.

I still remember the first time I stepped foot in Albania. I was filled with excitement, but also a lot of uncertainty. I did not know the language, I did not fully understand the culture, and I did not know what to expect from the people I would meet. But as I stepped off the plane and into this new chapter of my life, I felt a sense of peace. I knew that God had called me here, and even though I did not have all the answers, I was ready to trust Him and embrace the adventure He had laid out before me.

That is the thing about faith—it often calls us out of our comfort zones. Whether it is traveling to a new place, starting a new chapter in life, or simply stepping out to share your faith with someone, God often asks us to take risks, to be bold, and to trust Him in the unknown. And while that can be scary at times, it is also incredibly exciting.

One of the stories from the Bible that has always inspired me is the story of Abraham. In **Genesis 12:1**, God tells Abraham, "Go from your country, your people, and your father's household to the land I will show you." God did not give Abraham all the details—He simply told him to go. And Abraham, in faith, obeyed, trusting that God would guide him along the way. Abraham's journey was filled with both blessings and challenges, but through it all, God was with him, leading him into a life full of purpose and promise.

That same call is extended to each of us. God is inviting you on an adventure—an adventure of faith, where you will discover who He has called you to be, what He has planned for your life, and how He wants to use you to make a difference in the world. It will not always be easy. There will be moments when you feel unsure of the path ahead, when the challenges seem too big, or when you do not know if you have the strength to keep going. But I can promise you this: when you trust God, He will take you places you never thought possible, and your life will be filled with more adventure than you could ever imagine.

During my time in Finland, I experienced some of the hardest moments of my life. The culture was different, the language was hard to learn, and at times, I felt very alone. But it was during those moments of struggle that I learned to lean on God in a deeper way. I realized that part of embracing the adventure of faith is trusting that God is with you in both the high points and the low points. He does not just lead us into exciting unfamiliar places—He also walks with us through the valleys, giving us strength and courage when the journey feels difficult.

There were days in Finland when I was not sure I could keep going. I missed my home, my friends, and the familiarity of the places I had been before. But God was teaching me something important: adventure is not just about the exciting parts—it is also about perseverance, trust, and learning to rely on Him in every season of life.

I think about the apostle Paul, who faced incredible challenges during his ministry. He was shipwrecked, imprisoned, and faced persecution, but he never gave up. Why? Because he knew that the adventure of following God was worth it. In **2 Corinthians 12:9**, Paul writes, "But He said to me, 'My grace is sufficient for you, for My power is made perfect in weakness.'" Paul understood that even in his weakest moments, God was working through him, giving him the strength to keep going.

You might be wondering what kind of adventure God has planned for your life. Maybe you're still figuring out what your next steps should be, or maybe you have already felt God calling you to do something that feels big or intimidating. Whatever the case, I want to encourage you to say yes to God's adventure. It might take you places you never expected, and it might challenge you in ways you have never been challenged before, but I can promise you that it will be worth it.

One of the most exciting parts of following God is that He often surprises us with opportunities we never saw coming. During my time in ministry, I have had the chance to meet people from all walks of life, experience different cultures, and see firsthand how God is working around the world. None of that would have been possible if I had stayed in my comfort zone. It was only when I stepped out in faith and embraced the adventure that God was able to use me in ways I never expected.

And the same is true for you. God has a unique adventure planned for your life—one that is filled with purpose, meaning, and opportunities to make a difference. It will not always be easy, but it will be an adventure like no other.

Reflection Verse

"Have I not commanded you? Be strong and courageous. Do not be afraid; do not be discouraged, for the Lord your God will be with you wherever you go."

— Joshua 1:9 (NIV)

Reflection

What kind of adventure is God calling you to? Are there areas of your life where you feel hesitant or afraid to step out in faith? Remember that God promises to be with you wherever you go, and His grace is sufficient for every challenge you face.

Take a moment to think about what it means to embrace the adventure of following God. Where is He leading you? What steps of faith is He asking you to take? Trust that He will guide you and give you the courage to step into the unknown.

Prayer

Dear God,

Thank You for inviting me on an adventure of faith. Help me to trust You with every step of my journey, knowing that You are with me in both the exciting moments and the challenging ones. Give me the courage to embrace the adventure You have for my life, and remind me that I am never alone, because You are guiding me every step of the way. Amen.

Think about a time when you stepped out in faith and experienced something new or unexpected. How did it feel? Write about that experience in a journal and reflect on how God was with you during that adventure. Then, consider what adventure God might be calling you too next. How can you embrace it with courage and trust?

*Also, memorize **Joshua 1:9** and let it be a reminder that God will be with you in every adventure He calls you to.*

Chapter 15

TRUSTING GOD'S PLAN

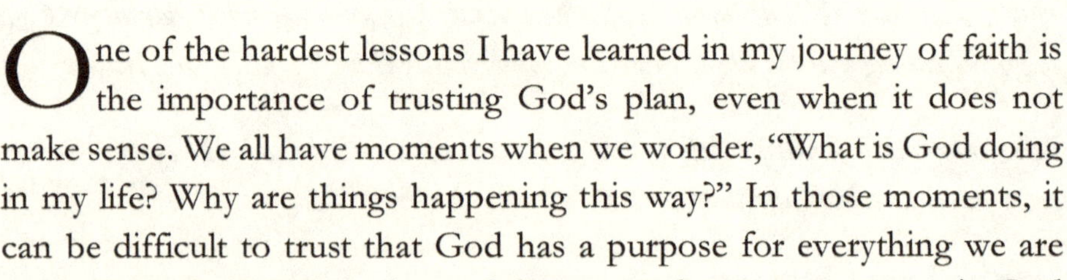

One of the hardest lessons I have learned in my journey of faith is the importance of trusting God's plan, even when it does not make sense. We all have moments when we wonder, "What is God doing in my life? Why are things happening this way?" In those moments, it can be difficult to trust that God has a purpose for everything we are going through, but I have learned that even when we cannot see it, God is working behind the scenes, weaving every part of our story together for His greater plan.

When I was younger, I had my own ideas about what my life would look like. I thought I had everything figured out. But as I started to follow God's call on my life, I realized that His plan was much different from mine—and far better than anything I could have imagined.

One of the biggest turning points in my life came when I felt God calling me to leave my home in Guyana and go on my first mission trip. It was exciting and a little overwhelming to think about leaving behind everything familiar, but I trusted that God had a plan for me. However, I quickly discovered that trusting God's plan did not mean everything would be easy.

When I arrived in Albania, I faced challenges I had not anticipated. I struggled with the language, I missed my family, and I often felt like I was completely out of my depth. There were moments when I questioned whether I had made the right decision. "God, why did You bring me here?" I would ask. "Is this really part of Your plan for me?"

During those difficult days, I found comfort in one of my favorite verses, **Jeremiah 29:11**, where God says, "For I know the plans I have for you, declares the Lord, plans to prosper you and not to harm you, plans to give you hope and a future." That verse reminded me that even when I did not understand what was happening, God had a plan, and it was a plan for my good.

It took time, but as I continued to serve in Albania, I began to see how God was working through the challenges I faced. I made deep, meaningful connections with people, and I saw lives transformed by the Gospel. God was using me in ways I had not expected, and through it all, He was teaching me to trust Him more deeply. Even though the road was not easy, I knew I was exactly where God wanted me to be.

One of the most powerful lessons I learned is that trusting God's plan means letting go of our need for control. We like to plan out our lives, to know what is coming next, and to feel like we are in control of our own destiny. But when we follow God, He often leads us in directions we never could have anticipated. It is in those moments, when we feel out of control, that we learn to truly trust Him.

I experienced this again when I moved to Finland. Once again, I found myself in a new country with a different language and culture. There were many days when I felt unsure of what God was doing. Why had He brought me here? What was His purpose for this season of my life?

But as time went on, I saw how God was opening doors and providing opportunities to share His love with people who had never heard the Gospel. I realized that trusting God's plan does not mean we always have all the answers—it means believing that He is guiding us, even when we do not know what is coming next.

In the Bible, one of the best examples of someone who trusted God's plan is Joseph. Joseph's life was full of unexpected twists and turns. He was sold into slavery by his own brothers, falsely accused of a crime he did not commit, and thrown into prison. It would have been easy for Joseph to give up and question why all these terrible things were happening to him. But Joseph never lost faith in God's plan.

In **Genesis 50:20,** Joseph says to his brothers, "You intended to harm me, but God intended it for good to accomplish what is now being done, the saving of many lives." Joseph understood that even though his circumstances were difficult, God was using them for a greater purpose. And in the end, Joseph's trust in God's plan allowed him to become a key figure in saving the lives of many people during a time of famine.

Like Joseph, we do not always know how our story will unfold. We may face hardships, disappointments, and moments of uncertainty, but when we trust God's plan, we can be confident that He is working all things together for good. Even the challenges we face are part of His greater purpose for our lives.

For young people like you, trusting God's plan might feel difficult at times, especially when life does not go the way you expected. Maybe you've faced setbacks in school, with friends, or in your personal life, and you are wondering why things are not working out the way you hoped. But I want to encourage you: God's plan for your life is bigger than any challenge you are facing right now. He sees the whole picture, and He knows what is best for you.

There will be times when you do not understand why things are happening the way they are. You might feel frustrated, confused, or even angry at God. But in those moments, I want you to remember that God's plan is always good, even when we do not see it. Trusting Him means believing that He is in control, and that He is leading you on a path that will bring you closer to Him.

In **Proverbs 3:5-6**, the Bible says, "Trust in the Lord with all your heart and lean not on your own understanding; in all your ways submit to Him, and He will make your paths straight." That verse has been a guiding light for me throughout my life. It reminds me that trusting God is not about having all the answers—it is about submitting to His will, even when I do not fully understand what He is doing.

Reflection Verse

"Trust in the Lord with all your heart and lean not on your own understanding; in all your ways submit to Him, and He will make your paths straight."

*— **Proverbs 3:5-6 (NIV)***

Reflection

Trusting God's plan can be hard, especially when life does not go the way we want it to. But the Bible reminds us that God's plan is always good, and that He is guiding us, even in the difficult moments. Take a moment to think about a time in your life when you had to trust God, even when you did not understand what was happening. How did God show His faithfulness to you in that situation?

What challenges are you facing right now where you need to trust God's plan? Ask Him to help you submit to His will and trust that He is working everything together for your good.

Prayer

Dear God, Thank You for having a plan for my life that is good, even when I do not always understand it. Help me to trust You in every circumstance, and to submit to

Your will, knowing that You are in control. When life feels uncertain, remind me that You are guiding my steps and that Your plan for me is filled with hope and a future.

Amen.

Think about a time in your life when things did not go the way you planned, but later on, you saw how God was working through it. Write about that experience in a journal and reflect on how it shaped your faith. Then, think about a current challenge you are facing, and ask God to help you trust His plan for that situation.

*Also, memorize **Proverbs 3:5-6** and let it be a reminder to trust God with all your heart, knowing that He will guide your path.*

Chapter 16

FINDING STRENGTH IN WEAKNESS

There is a saying that goes, "What doesn't kill you makes you stronger." While there's truth in that statement, I have learned through my own journey that true strength does not come from our ability to endure hard times alone. Real strength comes from recognizing our weakness and relying on God's power to carry us through.

One of the most significant lessons I have learned in my life is that God's strength often shows up in the moments when we feel the weakest. When everything seems to be falling apart, and we feel like we cannot go on, that's when God steps in and gives us the power to keep going.

There was a time during my ministry in Albania when I felt completely overwhelmed. I had been working non-stop, leading different ministries, teaching, and trying to build relationships in a new culture. At first, I was filled with energy and enthusiasm, but over time, the demands of the work began to wear me down. I found myself feeling physically exhausted, emotionally drained, and spiritually depleted.

I tried to push through it. I thought that if I just worked harder, prayed more, and stayed focused, I could handle it all. But instead of getting better, things got worse. I started to feel like I was failing—like I was not good enough to do the work God had called me to do. The more I tried to rely on my own strength, the more I realized how weak I really was.

One day, after a particularly challenging week, I found myself sitting alone, feeling completely empty. I had nothing left to give, and I was not sure how I could keep going. It was in that moment of weakness that I turned to God and prayed a simple prayer: "Lord, I cannot do this on my own. I need Your strength."

As I prayed, I felt a sense of peace wash over me. It was not a dramatic moment where everything suddenly got better, but I felt a quiet assurance that God was with me and that I did not have to rely on my own strength anymore. I realized that God was not asking me to be strong on my own—He was asking me to trust Him and allow His strength to work through me.

One of the most powerful verses in the Bible is **2 Corinthians 12:9**, where God says, "My grace is sufficient for you, for My power is made perfect in weakness." When the apostle Paul wrote those words, he was going through a tough time, too. He had prayed for God to remove a "thorn" from his life, but instead of taking it away, God reminded Paul that His grace was enough, and that His power would be revealed through Paul's weakness.

That verse has become a source of strength for me in my own life. It is a reminder that I do not have to be perfect. I do not have to have all the answers or be strong all the time. God's grace is enough, and His power is most evident when I recognize my need for Him.

Shortly after that prayer, something incredible happened. I started to see God's hand at work in ways I had not noticed before. I received unexpected help from others in the ministry. People began to step up and take on responsibilities that I had been carrying alone. I realized that

God was providing exactly what I needed—His strength, working through the people around me.

That experience taught me that it is okay to admit when we are struggling. It is okay to acknowledge our weakness because that's when God steps in and shows us His power. So often, we feel like we must be strong all the time, but the truth is, we were never meant to carry the weight of the world on our shoulders. God is our strength, and when we lean on Him, He gives us the power to do more than we ever could on our own.

For young people like you, it can be easy to feel like you have to be strong all the time. Maybe you feel pressure to succeed in school, to be a good friend, or to meet the expectations of others. Maybe you are going through something difficult, and you feel like you have to handle it on your own. But I want to encourage you: you do not have to be strong on your own. God's strength is available to you, and He is with you every step of the way.

In **Isaiah 40:29**, the Bible says, "He gives strength to the weary and increases the power of the weak." That verse reminds us that when we feel tired, worn out, or overwhelmed, God is ready to give us the strength we need. All we have to do is ask.

I have learned that true strength comes from surrendering our weakness to God. It is about letting go of our pride and admitting that we cannot do it all on our own. When we do that, God steps in and fills us with His power, giving us the strength to keep going, even when life gets tough.

Reflection Verse

*"But He said to me, 'My grace is sufficient for you, for My power is made perfect in weakness.' Therefore, I will boast all the more gladly about my weaknesses, so that Christ's power may rest on me." — **2 Corinthians 12:9 (NIV)***

Reflection

Have you ever felt like you had to be strong all the time? Maybe you've been trying to handle everything on your own, and it is left you feeling tired and overwhelmed. The Bible reminds us that we do not have to rely on our own strength—God's power is made perfect in our weakness. When we admit that we need His help, He gives us the strength we need to keep going.

Think about a time when you felt weak or overwhelmed. How did God show up in that moment? How can you rely on His strength in your life right now?

Prayer:

Dear God,

Thank You for reminding me that I do not have to be strong on my own. Help me to trust You with my weaknesses and to rely on Your strength in every situation. When I feel tired or overwhelmed, remind me that Your grace is enough and that Your power is made perfect in my weakness. Thank You for always being with me and giving me the strength I need.

Amen.

*Take a moment to think about an area of your life where you feel weak or overwhelmed. Write it down, and then spend some time in prayer, asking God to give you His strength in that situation. After you pray, read **2 Corinthians 12:9** again and reflect on what it means to rely on God's strength instead of your own.*

*Also, memorize **Isaiah 40:29**, and let it remind you that God gives strength to the weary and increases the power of the weak.*

Chapter 17

THE POWER OF PRAYER

There is one thing I have learned that has been essential in my life of faith—it is the power of prayer. Prayer is not just a ritual we do before meals or before bed. It is a direct line to God, a conversation that allows us to share our deepest thoughts, our struggles, our hopes, and even our fears. But it is more than that. Prayer is not just about talking to God—it is about listening to Him as well, learning to hear His voice, and understanding His heart for us.

One of the most significant moments in my life where I saw the power of prayer at work was during a mission trip to a remote village in Albania. We had planned a large outreach event in the village, hoping to share the Gospel with the local people, many of whom had never heard about Jesus before. As the day of the event approached, everything seemed to be falling apart. Our equipment was not working, the weather forecast predicted rain, and some members of our team were dealing with sickness. It felt like everything was going wrong, and we were all feeling discouraged.

But instead of giving in to defeat, our team gathered together to pray. We prayed for healing for those who were sick, for the weather to change, and for God to move in the hearts of the people we were about to meet. We prayed with boldness and faith, trusting that God could do the impossible, even in the face of overwhelming challenges.

And something incredible happened.

The very next morning, the weather cleared up, the equipment began working again, and those who had been sick were feeling better. We were able to hold the outreach event as planned, and it was a powerful time of ministry. Many people in the village gave their lives to Christ that day, and we were reminded once again that prayer has the power to change everything.

In **James 5:16**, the Bible says, "The prayer of a righteous person is powerful and effective." That verse has always been a reminder to me that prayer is not just something we do because we are supposed to—it is a powerful tool that can bring about real change. When we pray, we are inviting God to step into our situations, and we are acknowledging that we need His help and guidance.

But prayer is not just about asking God for things—it is also about building a relationship with Him. Prayer allows us to connect with God on a deeper level, to share our hearts with Him, and to hear what He has to say to us. There have been countless times in my life when I have felt lost or unsure about what to do next, and in those moments, prayer has been my lifeline. It is in those quiet moments of prayer that I have felt God's peace, His guidance, and His presence in a way that nothing else could provide.

One of the most transformative moments in my prayer life came during a particularly difficult season when I was feeling overwhelmed with responsibilities. The weight of ministry, personal struggles, and life in a foreign country felt like too much to handle. I found myself waking up each morning with a sense of dread, wondering how I was going to make it through the day.

In my desperation, I decided to dedicate more time to prayer. I began waking up early each morning and spending time alone with God. At first, I was not sure if it would make a difference, but as the days went by, something shifted inside me. The more time I spent in prayer, the more I began to feel God's presence and peace surrounding me. I did not have all the answers to my problems, but I knew that God was with me, and that gave me the strength to keep going.

Prayer became my source of strength, my refuge in times of trouble, and the way I connected with God on a deeper level. I learned that prayer is not about getting what we want—it is about aligning our hearts with God's will and trusting that He knows what is best for us.

Jesus Himself modeled the importance of prayer throughout His life. In **Luke 5:16**, it says, "But Jesus often withdrew to lonely places and prayed." Even though Jesus was the Son of God, He knew how important it was to spend time in prayer, seeking His Father's guidance and strength. If Jesus needed to pray, how much more do we need it in our lives?

One of the things I have learned is that prayer is not just for the big moments in life—it is for the small, everyday moments too. God wants us to talk to Him about everything, not just the major decisions or the crises we face. Whether we are struggling with a difficult decision, feeling anxious about the future, or simply needing encouragement, God is always ready to listen.

Sometimes, we might feel like our prayers are too small or insignificant for God to care about, but that is not true. God cares about every detail of our lives, and He wants us to bring everything to Him in prayer. **Philippians 4:6** reminds us, "Do not be anxious about anything, but in every situation, by prayer and petition, with thanksgiving, present your requests to God." That means we can pray about anything and everything, knowing that God is listening.

For young people like you, building a strong prayer life is one of the most important things you can do in your journey of faith. Prayer is how we stay connected to God, how we find strength in challenging times, and how we align our hearts with His will. It is through prayer that we grow in our relationship with Him, learning to trust Him more deeply with every aspect of our lives.

I want to encourage you to make prayer a regular part of your daily life. It does not have to be complicated—just start by talking to God like you would talk to a friend. Share what is on your heart, ask for His guidance, and listen for His voice. The more you pray, the more you will see how powerful and effective prayer can be.

Reflection Verse

"The prayer of a righteous person is powerful and effective."

— James 5:16 (NIV)

Reflection

What does your prayer life look like right now? Are there areas where you need to invite God's power to work in your life? Remember that prayer is not just something we do out of obligation—it is a way to connect with God, to seek His guidance, and to experience His presence in a deeper way.

Think about a time when you prayed about something and saw God work in that situation. How did it impact your faith? How can you grow in your prayer life today?

Prayer

Dear God, Thank You for the gift of prayer and for the incredible power that comes when we talk to You. Help me to make prayer a regular part of my life and teach me to trust You more deeply as I *seek Your will. Remind me that no prayer is too small for You and that You are always ready to listen. Thank You for hearing my prayers and for guiding me in every situation. Amen.*

Take sometime today to pray about something specific in your life. It could be a challenge you are facing, a decision you need to make, or something that has been weighing on your heart. Spend a few moments talking to God about it, and then take some time to listen for His voice. Write down what you feel God is saying to you and reflect on how you can trust Him in that situation.

*Also, memorize **James 5:16**, and let it remind you that your prayers are powerful and effective.*

Chapter 18

FINDING JOY IN EVERY SEASON

Life is full of ups and downs—moments of excitement and joy, and moments of difficulty and sorrow. But one of the most important lessons I have learned in my faith journey is that joy is not dependent on our circumstances. True joy comes from knowing God and trusting Him in every season of life.

There was a time during my missionary work in Albania when I struggled to find joy. Life felt heavy. The challenges of ministry, the difficulties of living in a foreign country, and the loneliness of being far from family weighed me down. It was a season where I felt drained—both physically and emotionally. Each day felt like a mountain to climb, and joy seemed distant.

But it was during that tough season that I learned a powerful lesson: joy does not always come from things going right; sometimes, joy is found in the midst of hardship, when we choose to trust God, even when life does not make sense. I discovered that joy is not about being happy all the time—it is about finding peace and contentment in God's presence, no matter what is happening around us.

One day, I was sitting in a small, quiet village in Albania, feeling overwhelmed by the weight of my responsibilities. I had just finished a long day of ministry, and I felt completely exhausted. I remember looking out at the mountains in the distance and feeling a sense of emptiness. I had given so much of myself to the work, but I felt like I had nothing left to give.

In that moment, I prayed, asking God to give me strength. And as I sat there, something unexpected happened. A sense of peace washed over me. I felt God reminding me that He was with me, that He had not forgotten me, and that He was my source of strength and joy. It was not a moment of loud celebration or overwhelming happiness, but it was a deep sense of joy that came from knowing that God was with me, even in the hard moments.

That experience reminded me of one of my favorite verses, **Nehemiah 8:10**, which says, "The joy of the Lord is your strength." That joy was not about everything going perfectly—it was about knowing that God's presence and love were enough to sustain me, even when I felt weak.

One of the things I have learned is that joy is a choice. It is easy to feel joyful when everything is going well, but the real test of joy comes when life is hard. Can we still find joy when things are not going our way? Can we trust that God is working behind the scenes, even when we cannot see the results yet?

Paul, one of the greatest missionaries in the Bible, understood this kind of joy. In **Philippians 4:4**, he writes, "Rejoice in the Lord always. I will say it again: Rejoice!" What is amazing about this verse is that Paul wrote it while he was in prison. He was not in a comfortable place; he was not surrounded by luxury or ease. He was in a dark, cold prison cell, yet he was able to say, "Rejoice in the Lord always." How could he say that? Because Paul's joy did not come from his circumstances—it came from his relationship with God.

I have found that when we focus on our problems, it is easy to feel discouraged. But when we focus on God and His goodness, we can find joy even in the trickiest situations. It is a shift in perspective. Instead of looking at what is wrong, we can choose to look at what is right—God's faithfulness, His promises, and His love for us.

One of the most joyful moments I have experienced came during a mission, where I had the opportunity to work with young people who had extraordinarily little in terms of material wealth. They lived in challenging circumstances, yet they had such a deep sense of joy. I remember seeing their smiles, hearing their laughter, and watching them worship God with all their hearts. It reminded me that joy is not about what we have—it is about who we know. And when we know God, we have every reason to be joyful, no matter what our circumstances look like.

For young people like you, life can sometimes feel overwhelming. You may face pressure from school, challenges with friends, or uncertainties about the future. It is easy to feel like joy is something that only comes when everything is going perfectly. But I want to encourage you: joy is available to you right now, in every season of life, because it comes from God.

In **Psalm 16:11**, the Bible says, "You make known to me the path of life; You will fill me with joy in Your presence, with eternal pleasures at Your right hand." That verse reminds us that real joy is found in God's presence. When we spend time with Him—through prayer, worship, and reading His Word—we are filled with a joy that goes beyond our circumstances.

One of the keys to finding joy in every season is gratitude. When we focus on what we are thankful for, we begin to see God's goodness in every part of our lives. Even in the difficult moments, there are always things to be grateful for—God's love, His provision, His guidance, and the people He is placed in our lives.

During my toughest moments, I have learned to make a habit of gratitude. I start my day by thanking God for His blessings, even when I do not feel like it. I thank Him for His faithfulness, for His presence, and for the little things that often go unnoticed. And as I do, I find that my perspective shifts. Instead of focusing on what is wrong, I start to see what is right. And in that place of gratitude, joy begins to grow.

I want to encourage you to practice gratitude in your own life. Take time each day to thank God for His goodness, even when life feels hard. When you do, you will begin to experience the joy that comes from knowing that God is with you in every season.

Reflection Verse

"The joy of the Lord is your strength."

— *Nehemiah 8:10 (NIV)*

Reflection

Think about a time in your life when you found joy, even when things were hard. What was it that brought you that joy? How did it change your perspective on your situation? The Bible reminds us that the joy of the Lord is our strength, meaning that we can find strength in the joy that comes from knowing God is with us, no matter what we are facing.

What are you thankful for right now? How can you focus on God's goodness in your life, even if you are going through a tough time?

Prayer

Dear God, Thank You for the joy that comes from knowing You. Help me to find joy in every season of life, even when things are hard. Remind me that true joy does not come from my circumstances but from Your presence. Teach me to be grateful for all the ways You are working in my life and help me to trust You with every part of my journey.

Amen.

Take a few moments today to write down three things you are thankful for. They can be big things or trivial things but focus on how God has blessed you. After you write them down, spend some time in prayer, thanking God for His goodness in your life.

Also, memorize **Nehemiah 8:10**, *and let it remind you that the joy of the Lord is your strength, no matter what season you are in.*

Chapter 19

STANDING FIRM IN FAITH

One of the most important lessons I have learned on my journey of faith is how to stand firm, even when life feels uncertain or when others challenge what I believe. Standing firm in faith does not mean that life will always be easy. In fact, sometimes standing for what you believe in will bring opposition or trials, but it is in those moments that God gives us the strength to hold our ground.

There was a particular moment during my missionary work in Albania when I had to learn how to stand firm in my faith. At the time, Albania was a country still finding its way after years of communist rule, where religion had been outlawed. The idea of Christianity was foreign to many, and as a missionary, I faced resistance. Some people were skeptical, and others were outright hostile to the message I was sharing.

One afternoon, I was invited to speak at a community gathering in a village where people were not incredibly open to outsiders or to hearing about Christianity. As I arrived, I could sense that some were curious, but others were already set on rejecting whatever I had to say. There was a group of men at the back of the room who seemed determined to cause disruption. As I began to speak about Jesus and the hope we have in Him, I could feel the tension in the room growing.

At that moment, I could have chosen to hold back, to soften the message, or to avoid saying anything that might upset the people who were clearly against me. But deep inside, I knew that God had called me to be bold in sharing His love, no matter the response. So, I stood firm. I spoke the truth with love, sharing my testimony and explaining how Jesus had transformed my life.

As I continued, I noticed that the men who had been so vocal at the beginning grew quieter. They were not necessarily convinced, but something in their demeanor changed. After the meeting, one of the men approached me. He did not accept Christ that day, but he did thank me for being courageous enough to speak honestly. He told me that he had never heard anyone talk about faith in such a personal way before. It was a small sign that God was at work, even in a place where I thought my message might not be welcome.

This experience reminded me of the importance of standing firm in faith, even when it is uncomfortable or when others seem opposed to what we believe. It is not always about seeing immediate results, but about being faithful to God's calling, trusting that He is working in ways we cannot always see.

The Bible tells us in **Ephesians 6:13**, "Therefore put on the full armor of God, so that when the day of evil comes, you may be able to stand your ground, and after you have done everything, to stand." This verse encourages us to be prepared for the challenges that will come. It is not a matter of if we will face opposition, but when. And when that time comes, God equips us with everything we need to stand firm in our faith.

One of the most powerful examples of standing firm in faith comes from the story of Daniel. In **Daniel 6**, we read about how Daniel continued to pray to God, even though the king had issued a decree forbidding prayer to anyone but the king himself. Daniel could have easily stopped praying to avoid getting into trouble, but he chose to stand firm in his faith, trusting that God would protect him. As a result, when Daniel was thrown into the lion's den, God sent an angel to shut the mouths of the lions, and Daniel was unharmed. His unwavering faith became a powerful testimony to the king and those around him.

Standing firm in faith might mean standing up for your beliefs at school, with friends, or even at home. It might mean resisting the temptation to go along with what everyone else is doing, even when it is easier to fit in. But when we stand firm in our faith, we show others that our trust is in God, and that we believe He will carry us through whatever challenges we face.

Reflection Verse

"Therefore, put on the full armor of God, so that when the day of evil comes, you may be able to stand your ground, and after you have done everything, to stand."

*— **Ephesians 6:13 (NIV)***

Reflection

Think about a time when your faith was challenged—either by circumstances or by people around you. How did you respond? Did you feel like you could stand firm in your beliefs, or was it difficult to hold your ground? The Bible reminds us that standing firm is not something we do in our own strength—it is something God enables us to do when we rely on Him.

In your current situation, is there an area where you need to stand firm in your faith? How can you trust God to give you the strength and courage to do so?

Prayer

Dear God,

Thank You for giving me the strength to stand firm in my faith. Help me to trust You in every situation, even when I feel unsure or afraid. Teach me to rely on Your power and to put on the full armor of God, so that I can stand strong, no matter what challenges I face. Thank You for being with me and guiding me every step of the way.

Amen.

Take a moment to think about an area in your life where your faith is being tested. It could be something at school, with your friends, or even in your personal life. Write down how you are feeling and what you think God is asking you to do. Then, spend some time in prayer, asking God to help you stand firm in your faith and trust Him through it all.

Also, memorize **Ephesians 6:13**, *and let it remind you that God gives you the strength to stand firm, no matter what comes your way.*

Chapter 20

WALKING BOLDLY INTO GOD'S FUTURE

As we come to the end of this book, I want to remind you of something important: this is not the end of your journey—it is just the beginning.

Walking with God is a lifelong adventure, full of twists and turns, challenges, and victories. No matter where you are right now in your faith journey, God has an amazing future planned for you. It may not always be easy, and there will be times when you face uncertainty, but I want to encourage you to step boldly into the future, trusting that God is leading the way.

One of the greatest lessons I have learned is that God's plans for our lives are bigger and better than anything we could ever imagine. When I first gave my life to Christ as a young boy in Guyana, I never could have predicted all the places He would take me. From the remote villages of Albania to the snowy landscapes of Finland, from moments of triumph to seasons of deep struggle, every step of the way, God has been faithful.

There is a verse in the Bible that has always reminded me of this truth. **Jeremiah 29:11** says, "For I know the plans I have for you," declares the Lord, "plans to prosper you and not to harm you, plans to give you hope and a future." This verse has been a guiding light for me, especially during times when I was not sure what the future held. It is a reminder that God sees the bigger picture, even when we do not, and that His plans are always for our good.

One of the most powerful moments in my journey happened when I was at a crossroads, unsure of what God wanted me to do next. I had just finished a season of ministry that had been both exhausting and rewarding, and I felt like I was standing at the edge of a cliff, looking out at a future I could not fully see. There were doors opening in different directions, but I did not know which one to walk through. In my confusion, I turned to God in prayer, asking Him to guide my steps.

And in that moment, I felt God's peace wash over me, reminding me that I did not have to have all the answers right away. I just needed to take the next step of faith, trusting that He would lead me where I needed to go. I realized that walking boldly into God's future is not about knowing everything in advance—it is about trusting God with each step, one at a time.

Maybe you're in a place right now where you are unsure of what is next. Maybe you're wondering what God's plan is for your life, or you are facing a decision that feels overwhelming. I want to encourage you to take a deep breath and trust that God has already gone ahead of you. He knows the way, and He will guide you, just as He has guided me through every season of my life.

Throughout this book, we have talked about hearing God's call, standing firm in faith, and trusting Him through challenges. Now, as we look to the future, I want you to remember that the same God who has walked with you through the past will continue to walk with you into the future.

Walking boldly into God's future does not mean we will not face obstacles. In fact, there will be times when the road ahead looks difficult, and we may be tempted to turn back. But it is in those moments that we need to hold onto God's promises. He never promised that the journey would be easy, but He did promise that He would never leave us or forsake us.

One of the most memorable experiences I had during my time as a missionary was watching young people step out in faith for the first time. I have seen teenagers in Albania and Finland take bold steps to share their faith with others, even when they were scared or unsure. I have watched as they grew in confidence, knowing that God was with them. It reminded me that faith is not about having everything figured out—it is about trusting God enough to take the next step, even when we cannot see the whole picture.

That is what I want to leave you with as we close this book: the encouragement to walk boldly into the future God has for you. You do not have to know all the answers. You do not have to have everything figured out. You just need to trust that God's plans for you are good, and that He will guide you every step of the way.

In **Proverbs 3:5-6**, the Bible says, "Trust in the Lord with all your heart and lean not on your own understanding; in all your ways submit to Him, and He will make your paths straight." This verse has been an anchor for me, reminding me that I do not have to rely on my own understanding. When I submit my life to God and trust Him with my future, He will make the path clear.

So, as you move forward in your own journey, I encourage you to trust God with every part of your life. Whether you are making decisions about your future, facing challenges, or simply trying to grow in your faith, know that God is with you. He has incredible plans for your life— plans that are bigger than anything you could imagine.

Reflection Verse

"For I know the plans I have for you," declares the Lord, "plans to prosper you and not to harm you, plans to give you hope and a future."

— Jeremiah 29:11 (NIV)

Reflection

As you think about your future, what are some of the dreams and goals you have? How can you trust God with those plans, even if you are not sure how everything will work out? Remember that God has a plan for your life, and He will guide you every step of the way.

What are some areas in your life where you need to take a step of faith? How can you trust God more deeply with your future, knowing that His plans for you are good?

Prayer

Dear God,

Thank You for the incredible plans You have for my life. Help me to trust You with my future, knowing that You are leading the way. Give me the courage to take bold steps of faith, even when I do not have all the answers. Thank You for being with me in every season of my life, and for the amazing things You have in store for me.

Amen.

Take a few moments to write down your hopes and dreams for the future. These could be big goals, like what you want to do when you grow up, or smaller things, like how you want to grow in your faith. After you write them down, pray over each one, asking God to guide you as you move forward.

Also, memorize **Jeremiah 29:11**, *and let it remind you that God's plans for your life are good, and that He will guide you into a future full of hope.*

As we close this chapter and this book, I want to thank you for taking this journey with me. My prayer for you is that you will continue to walk boldly with God, trusting Him with every part of your life. The adventure is just beginning, and I cannot wait to see all the amazing things God has in store for you!

With love and blessings,

Cleon Alleyne

PRACTICAL STEPS FOR MOVING FORWARD

The following are some practical steps that can help you move forward, grow in your faith, and continue to walk closely with God.

1. Reflect on Your Journey

Take a moment to look back at the experiences, challenges, and victories you have encountered in your life. How has God been shaping you through these moments? What have you learned about His character and His plans for you? Reflecting on your journey is an important part of recognizing God's presence in your life and understanding where He may be leading you next.

Action Step: Set aside some quiet time to journal about your life's journey. Ask yourself: "Where has God shown His faithfulness to me? In what areas do I need to trust Him more?"

2. Identify Areas for Growth

None of us have "arrived" in our walk with God. There are always areas in our lives where we can grow—whether it is in trust, patience, compassion, or sharing our faith. As you reflect on your experiences, consider the areas where God may be calling you to grow deeper. It could be your prayer life, your relationships with others, or your willingness to step out in faith.

Action Step: Write down at least two areas where you feel God is calling you to grow. Set a goal for how you will take small, intentional steps to develop in those areas over the next few months.

3. Start Journaling

Journaling is a powerful tool to track your spiritual growth, express your prayers, and document how God is working in your life. It helps you stay grounded in gratitude and provides clarity during times of confusion or doubt. When you write down your thoughts and prayers, you create a

personal record of your journey with God, which you can look back on during challenging times.

Action Step: Begin a daily or weekly journaling practice. You do not have to write pages—just a few sentences about what God is teaching you, what you are grateful for, or the challenges you are facing. Over time, this will become a valuable reflection of your growth in faith.

4. Get Connected: Join a Small Group or Church Community

Growth happens best in community. Whether you are just starting your faith journey or have been walking with Jesus for years, being part of a small group or church community provides encouragement, accountability, and support. These connections help you grow by surrounding you with people who can pray for you, offer wisdom, and walk alongside you as you take steps of faith.

Action Step: If you are not already part of a small group or church community, take the first step by reaching out to a local church or ministry. Find a group of believers who are committed to growing together, praying for one another, and studying God's Word.

5. Serve and Volunteer

One of the most fulfilling ways to grow in faith is by serving others. Whether it is volunteering at your local church, helping at a community center, or reaching out to someone in need, serving shifts your focus from your own challenges to the needs of others. It is through serving that we experience God's heart for people and begin to see how our lives can make a difference.

Action Step: Look for opportunities to volunteer, whether in your local community or within your church. Pray about where God may be calling you to serve and step out in faith by offering your time and skills to bless others.

6. Share God's Love with Others

One of the greatest calls we have as followers of Christ is to share God's love with others. It does not have to be complicated—sometimes it is as simple as a conversation, a kind word, or an act of generosity. There may be someone in your life right now who needs to hear about the hope and love you have found in Christ. Pray for boldness and ask God to lead you to opportunities to share your faith.

Action Step: Think of one person in your life who could benefit from hearing about God's love. Pray for them and look for a way to reach out—whether through a conversation, an invitation to church, or a simple act of kindness.